American Counterinsurgency

American Counterinsurgency:
Human Science and the Human Terrain

Roberto J. González

PRICKLY PARADIGM PRESS
CHICAGO

Prickly Paradigm Press, LLC
5629 South University Avenue
Chicago, Il 60637

www.prickly-paradigm.com

ISBN-10: 0-9794057-4-2
ISBN-13: 978-0-9794057-4-7
LCCN: 2008937607

Printed in the United States of America on acid-free paper.

Table of Contents

His disciples have learned all too literally the instrumental attitude toward life, and, being immensely intelligent and energetic, they are making themselves efficient instruments of the war technique, accepting with little question the ends as announced from above.

—Randolph Bourne, *Twilight of Idols* (1917)

Preface

Kwame Nkrumah, the first prime minister and president of Ghana, possessed an enormous painting that hung in his foyer in the years following his country's independence from British colonial rule in 1957. The painting depicts a massive black human figure, breaking chains of bondage as lightning tears across the sky and the earth trembles. In the foreground, three small, pallid men flee in terror: a colonial administrator, carrying a briefcase; a Christian missionary, cradling the Bible; and an anthropologist, holding a book entitled *African Political Systems*.

The painting dramatically illustrated European social scientists who tainted themselves by collaborating with and participating in a brutal system that siphoned gold, diamonds, ivory, copper, and other riches from the so-called "Dark Continent." For decades, many colonial anthropologists sought to help administrators control native peoples. Yet their work denied from the outset the possibility of Africans' independence, autonomy, or self-determination. Instead, they sought to co-opt local leaders into a system of indirect rule, transforming them into puppets of colonial administrators. As the result of such work anthropology was virtually banned from independent Africa in the post-colonial period.

Today, a new group of social scientists has appeared in Iraq and Afghanistan. Most are known as "cultural analysts" and are members of "Human Terrain Teams" (HTTs)—combined civilian-military units embedded with US Army combat brigades for counterinsurgency (counter-guerrilla) warfare. Their work is geared towards helping brigade commanders use "cultural knowledge" as a tool for combat—and conquest.

Retired US Army General Robert Scales recently called the "war on terror" a "social scientists' war," implying that culture itself will become a critical weapon on the contemporary battlefield. In so doing, he pronounced the exact words of former Secretary of Defense Robert McNamara, who more than a generation ago referred to the US invasion of Vietnam as a "social scientists' war." Despite many problems associated with the use of such experts in Vietnam, neither Scales nor the directors of the Human Terrain System program (HTS) have adequately addressed the ethical quandaries of a new "social scientists' war."

From one perspective, social scientists' participation in HTS signals a radical shift in the "war on terror." As neoconservative architects of the wars in

Afghanistan and Iraq (Paul Wolfowitz, Douglas Feith, Richard Perle, Donald Rumsfeld, George Tenet) began dropping out of influential positions within the Bush administration, a new more pragmatic group began to assume their roles, led by Defense Secretary Robert Gates. On the military side, the new "liberal" approach to war fighting was embodied in the promotion of General David Petraeus to the position of top commander in Iraq (in January 2007), and later to the position of top commander of CENTCOM (Central Command).

From another perspective, HTS hearkens back to an earlier time in world history—the age of Euro-American empire. Like their 19th and 20th century predecessors in British Africa, French Indochina, and the United States, today's militarized social scientists are enmeshed in a modern-day mission to bring civilization, enlightenment, and "freedom" to the natives. Yet the nature of HTS—which requires its participants to surrender their autonomy to the military chain of command—jeopardizes the safety of Iraqis, Afghans, and American social scientists around the world.

How did this situation come to pass so quickly, in light of past failures? What efforts are underway to challenge these potentially malignant collaborations? What does the future hold for the growing militarization of the social sciences? This book is dedicated to a critical exploration of these and other questions that will shape the scientific world for years to come.

When I began studying cultural anthropology 15 years ago, I was enchanted by the possibility of learning from the lives of others. My interests inspired me to live among Zapotec farmers in the mountains of the southern Mexican state of Oaxaca for more than two years, where I was humbled by the vast agricultural and ecological knowledge of local villagers. As I struggled to keep up with the daily routine of farm life in the fragrant maize fields and lush coffee orchards of the sierra, I could not have imagined that one day, the US Foreign Military Studies Office would be funding social science research on "human terrain" in the same region of Oaxaca, or that the Department of Defense would be aggressively recruiting anthropologists to work alongside soldiers fighting on distant battlefields.

This book is about the development of an idea—human terrain—and how it has been transformed over the years. It is also about the most concrete consequence of that idea, namely the HTS program. Although I originally planned to write it as a way of uncovering more about the "human terrain" concept, it gradually became a critique of current trends in American social science, and in a broader sense a criticism of US foreign policy. If at times my words carry traces of bitterness, it is unintentional. It is also unwarranted. For too long I delayed examining the roots of my own discipline and the history of our country's dealings in the world, and my relatively recent efforts to learn more give me little satisfaction. I hope that my work will make a small contribution towards a more lucid understanding of these issues.

Chapter 1
The Myth of a "Gentler"
Counterinsurgency

Be polite, be professional, be prepared to kill.
— US Army Lieutenant Colonel John Nagl,
The Daily Show with Jon Stewart
(August 23, 2007)

To make sense of the world we live in, a historian once said, one must begin with the supposition that everything is topsy-turvy. The wrong people are in jail, while the wrong people are out of jail. The wrong people hold power, while the wrong people are without power. The wrong people are dispossessed of land and livelihoods, while the wrong people possess more land and riches than they will ever need.

If we start with this supposition, perhaps we can begin to make sense of how some psychologists, trained to help ease the suffering of others, are participating in the interrogation of prisoners at Guantánamo Bay—interrogations that have involved the application of torture. Perhaps we can begin to make sense of how some political scientists, whose work involves the analysis of democratic systems, recently formulated plans to overthrow sovereign governments abroad. Perhaps too we can begin to make sense of how some anthropologists, trained to learn about and empathize with people in other soci-

eties, are engaged in counterinsurgency work supporting an illegal occupation of foreign lands.

Between July 2005 and August 2006, the US Army
assembled an experimental program called the "Human
Terrain System" (HTS). It is part of a much broader
counterinsurgency effort designed to crush, suppress,
and smother resistance movements in occupied Iraq
and Afghanistan.

The program's building blocks are five-person
teams ("Human Terrain Teams" or HTTs) embedded
with combat brigades in Iraq and Afghanistan, which
include regional studies experts and social scientists.
Some of the social scientists are armed. There are five
HTTs in Iraq and one and Afghanistan, and approximately 20 more teams have been scheduled for deployment.

Some proponents insist that HTTs serve as "an
angel on the shoulder" of brigade leaders, since they
"provide commanders with knowledge about the local
societies... in order to get the effects on the population
that they want." Others emphasize the humanitarian
role of HTTs by claiming that they are building health
clinics, remodeling schools, or repairing mosques to
win Iraqi and Afghan hearts and minds. Dozens of
news reports in the corporate media have breathlessly
echoed these statements while downplaying or ignoring the ethical dilemmas inherent in such work. The
reports have uncritically accepted the Pentagon's
portrayal of the program as a life-saving success story,
and they have all the appearance of a highly orches-
trated public relations campaign.

The way in which HTS has been packaged—as
a kinder, gentler counterinsurgency—is completely

unsupported by evidence. HTS supporters frequently assert that the program has drastically reduced US "kinetic operations" (military attacks) in Afghanistan, but Pentagon officials haven't responded to requests for data to back up such claims. Indeed, there is no verifiable evidence that HTTs have saved a single life—American, Afghan, Iraqi or otherwise. Zenia Helbig (a former HTT member) has noted that an internal evaluation team that recently produced a positive report on HTS included evaluators with a vested interest in the program's continuation. (The report has not been made available to the public.)

Complicating matters further is the fact that HTT members are contractors to the US military. They are recruited and trained by a private corporation (BAE Systems, one of Europe's largest military contractors), which is responsible for paying their salaries. As private contractors, they are not subject to the Uniform Code of Military Justice (UCMJ), the foundation of military law.

A careful review of HTS indicates that the program, like many counterinsurgency initiatives, has at least two faces: one designed to rally public support for an increasingly unpopular war by displaying an enlightened approach to war fighting, and the other to collect new forms of intelligence to help salvage a failing occupation.

HTS represents a subversion of social science because it puts at risk Afghans and Iraqis who share information about their lives with embedded social scientists. Brigade commanders to whom HTT members are assigned can use data to create culturally specific propaganda campaigns, co-opt local leaders, or target suspected enemies for abduction or assassination.

It plays into the worst tradition of social science as a "handmaiden of colonialism."

CORDS for the 21st Century

If history is any guide, HTS was created primarily as a tool for espionage and intelligence gathering. As the Pentagon launched the program, military analysts with knowledge of HTS planning and implementation described it as a "CORDS for the 21st Century," in reference to Civil Operations and Revolutionary Development Support—a Vietnam War-era effort implemented jointly by US Military Assistance Command personnel and the government of South Vietnam. CORDS integrated military and civilian

Figure 1. US Army Major Robert Holbert speaks with local school administrators during a cordon and search of Nani, Afghanistan in June 2007. Holbert is a human terrain team member attached to the 4th Brigade Combat Team, 82nd Airborne Division. (Photo courtesy of US Army.)

teams dedicated to "pacification" of insurgent areas. (Typically civilians came from the State Department, US Agency for International Development, or other government agencies.) This was done on multiple fronts: US advisors trained South Vietnamese militias to fight Viet Cong (communist) sympathizers; hundreds of millions of dollars were distributed for medical, agricultural, and educational programs to win the allegiance of villagers throughout the country; and anti-communist propaganda was widely distributed in an aggressive psychological operations campaign.

CORDS also gave birth to the infamous Phoenix Program, a secret initiative in which CIA agents, US Special Forces, South Vietnamese military, and "Provincial Reconnaissance Units" (CIA mercenaries) attempted to root out members of the "Viet Cong infrastructure," nearly all of whom were civilians: Communist Party members, National Liberation Front cadres, and sympathetic villagers. In practice, Phoenix led to the capture, torture, and assassination (euphemistically called "neutralization" by the Pentagon) of tens of thousands of civilians. At the time, the Pentagon hailed CORDS as a humanitarian project for winning Vietnamese hearts and minds. However, the Phoenix Program simultaneously functioned as its paramilitary arm, replete with death squads that exterminated approximately 26,000 Vietnamese.

Perhaps nowhere was the goal of Phoenix more bluntly stated than in US Military Assistance Command Directive 381-41, which brought the program into being: it describes the program as a "rifle shot rather than a shotgun approach to the real target— the important political leaders and activists in the VC

[Viet Cong] infrastructure." This fit within the larger CORDS objective:

> To gather human and cultural intelligence and to develop economic and social programs... [and] to undermine support for the communist forces... A key feature leading to the success of CORDS was an effective information collection and reporting system that focused on factors essential for the promotion of security, economic development, governance, and the provision of needed government services down to the hamlet level.

CORDS thus relied heavily upon local intelligence gathered by "Revolutionary Development" and "Census Grievance" teams that built rapport with villagers, providing them with educational, medical,

Figure 2. Officers at the US Army's Foreign Military Studies Office draw comparisons between HTS and the Vietnam War-era CORDS/Phoenix program. Here suspected Viet Cong cadres are detained by CORDS/Phoenix personnel, circa 1968. (Photo courtesy of Texas Tech University Vietnam Archive.)

and agricultural development funds. The teams prepared ethnographic reports that included intelligence information which was then collected, collated, computerized, and used to create Phoenix blacklists. The paramilitary side of CORDS became the prototype for CIA-sponsored death squads in El Salvador, Honduras, and other countries where "dirty wars" were fought in the second half of the 20th century.

This history provides a critical reference point for understanding the potential uses—and abuses—of HTS. Though the program's boosters have portrayed it as an initiative that is improving the cultural awareness of soldiers in Iraq and Afghanistan, and as a humanitarian mission providing medical services and job training programs, we should bear in mind that the data collected by HTTs can serve functions far beyond these domains. For example, US Army officer Ken Tovo writes about how human terrain information will help target suspected "militant Islamic infrastructure": he enthusiastically speculates about how "a modern-day Phoenix Program" will help "neutralize the militant Islamic infrastructure (MI2) that enables the global insurgency" in Iraq and elsewhere, while ignoring the fact that Phoenix led to war crimes.

Interviews that I conducted with current and former HTS employees reveal that the program is being grossly mismanaged, which raises doubts about the security of HTT data—and consequently, the safety of Iraqis and Afghans who have provided information to team members.

The Rise of the Warrior-Intellectuals

The creation of HTS coincides with a broad shift within the Pentagon—the rise to power of a "small band of warrior-intellectuals" (in the words of the *Washington Post*) in the post-Rumsfeld era, led by US Army General David Petraeus. Petraeus, who has a PhD in international relations from Princeton, convened a team of social scientists who rose to prominence as the Bush administration desperately sought to improve the situation in Iraq. Among the most influential members of Petraeus' inner circle are Lieutenant Colonel David H. Kilcullen, an Australian who holds a PhD in politics from the University of New South Wales; Lieutenant Colonel John Nagl, who holds a PhD in history from Oxford's St. Anthony's College; Colonel Michael J. Meese, who holds a PhD in economics from Princeton; and Colonel Peter Mansoor, who holds a PhD in history from Ohio State University.

Defense Secretary Robert Gates (Rumsfeld's successor)—who himself has a PhD in history from Georgetown—gave a November 2007 speech in which he committed himself to "soft power... beyond the guns and steel of the military." He proposed increasing economic development aid, providing basic services to Iraqis and Afghans, and arming and training indigenous military units. Several months later, Gates proposed the "Minerva Consortium," an initiative designed to provide $100 million for university-based social science research geared towards meeting the Pentagon's needs. As evidence of fruitful collaboration between the Pentagon and social scientists, he portrayed the HTS program in glowing terms, describing it as a "key to long term success" in Iraq, Afghanistan, and beyond. Such ideas fit squarely within the Petraeus paradigm.

The "warrior-intellectuals" depart from the Pentagon's conventional wisdom in several ways. For example, in writing about counterinsurgency, Petraeus' associates have encouraged troops to "lighten their combat loads and enforce a habit of speed and mobility," advocated "building trusted networks" by "conducting village and neighborhood surveys to identify community needs," and suggested that soldiers "win the confidence of a few villages, and then work with those with whom they trade, intermarry, or do business." David Kilcullen, who is among the best-known of the "Petraeus boys," has suggested that military commanders and counterinsurgents "engage the women; be cautious around the children," since enemies might use youngsters as spies, and that "co-opting neutral or friendly women through targeted social and economic programs" might effectively disrupt terrorist networks. In a 2004 essay, Kilcullen went so far as to recommend that US forces initiate a "global 'Phoenix Program'" against an "Islamist insurgency." In a complete whitewash of Phoenix war crimes, he insisted that

> the unfairly maligned (but highly effective) Vietnam-era Phoenix program... was largely a civilian aid and development program, supported by targeted military pacification operations and intelligence activity to disrupt the Viet Cong Infrastructure.

The corporate media showered the soldier-scholars with lavish praise following the release of the US Army's new counterinsurgency manual, *FM 3-24*, the first of its kind in more than 20 years. The fact that *Time* magazine could describe *FM 3-24* as "radical," "revolutionary," and "Zen tinged" is a sobering reminder of a reactionary mass media and perhaps an increasingly apathetic (or gullible) public. Such descriptions accurately reflect the liberal end of the US political spectrum and provide insight into our country's militarized mass culture.

The University of Chicago Press reprinted the manual with an introduction by Sarah Sewall of Harvard University's Kennedy School of Government. (Sewall, who directs the Carr Center for Human Rights Policy, has become something of a poster child for a softer, more academically oriented approach to counterinsurgency.) The University of Chicago Press edition was clad in an olive-drab book jacket and received adulatory praise from *The New York Times* ("landmark," "paradigm-shattering"), the *Los Angeles Times* ("nifty"), and the *Chicago Tribune* ("probably the most important piece of doctrine written over the last 20 years").

Soon after the release of the Chicago edition, anthropologist David Price discovered that extensive portions of a key chapter of the book (Chapter 3) were plagiarized. In approximately 20 cases, the chapter's authors (anthropologist Montgomery McFate and a military intelligence officer) had lifted passages verbatim from several scholars including anthropologists Victor Turner, Fred Plog, and Daniel Bates and sociologists Max Weber and Anthony Giddens, with no attribution whatsoever. Lieutenant Colonel John Nagl rushed to McFate's defense in the online *Small Wars Journal*, noting:

> Field Manuals have their own grammar and their own logic. They are not doctoral dissertations, designed to be read by few and judged largely for the quality of their sourcing; instead, they are intended for use by soldiers. Thus authors are not named.

In response, Price noted that more than 100 sources were named in *FM 3-24*'s reference section, yet none corresponded to the pilfered passages. To this day, McFate has not made a public statement addressing the matter, nor has University of Chicago Press, who apparently rushed the handbook into publication without the normal peer review process (in which scholars assess the quality of the work). After the plagiarism fiasco, none of those who gave glowing evaluations of *FM 3-24* withdrew their praise.

These developments have been accompanied by expanding relationships between military think tanks and social scientists. For example, the US Army War College's Strategic Studies Institute recently sponsored a study by anthropologist Sheila Miyoshi Jager, an uncritical advocate of "gentler" counterinsurgency:

> In sharp contrast to former Secretary of Defense Donald Rumsfeld's heavy-handed approach to counterinsurgency which emphasized aggressive military tactics, the post-Rumsfeld Pentagon has advocated a "gentler" approach, emphasizing cultural knowledge and ethnographic intelligence... This "cultural turn" within DoD highlights efforts to understand adversary societies and to recruit "practitioners" of

culture, notably anthropologists, to help in the war effort in both Iraq and Afghanistan.

(Such passages provide a window into the world view of the counterinsurgent: "gentle" refers to gathering "ethnographic intelligence" on "adversary societies" for "the war effort.")

Many warrior-intellectuals fail to understand that the very idea of a "gentler" counterinsurgency— once called "counter-revolutionary" and "counter-guerrilla" operations—is a myth and a fantasy. Neil Whitehead reminds us that over time, counterinsurgents tend to mirror their enemies:

> Counterinsurgency campaigns tend to proceed by exactly the same kinds of military ploys that are being used by their terrorist enemies. So the selective assassination of individuals, the planting of particular kinds of bomb, or the the mining of particular kinds of places which are heavily used by civilians even if they are at the same time being used by terrorists—these are all ways in which the military activity of the state, as it engages with a terrorist enemy, itself becomes more like terrorism.

All modern counterinsurgency campaigns—including those conducted in Guatemala, South Vietnam, Algeria, Northern Ireland, East Timor, Chile, and Argentina to name but a few—have led to torture, mass murder, and state terror directed against civilians. Counterinsurgency efforts in Afghanistan and Iraq will lead to similar results if history is any guide.

HTS and the Mighty Wurlitzer

The earliest mention of HTS in a major US publication occurred late in 2006, when the *New Yorker* briefly mentioned it in an article entitled, "Knowing the Enemy." The piece included a reverent review of social scientists' collaboration with the Pentagon in the "war on terror," and described HTS as:

> a new project with the quintessential Pentagon name Cultural Operations Research Human Terrain. It began in the form of a "ruggedized" laptop computer, loaded with data from social-science research conducted in Iraq—such as, [Montgomery] McFate said, "an analysis of the eighty-eight tribes and subtribes in a particular province." Now the project is recruiting social scientists around the country to join five-person "human terrain" teams that would go to Iraq and Afghanistan with combat brigades and serve as cultural advisers on six-to-nine-month tours.

This piece was followed several months later with a lengthy profile of Montgomery McFate—a key architect of HTS—in the *San Francisco Chronicle Magazine*. The sympathetic article, cleverly tailored for a liberal Bay Area audience, portrayed McFate as a former punk rocker "with a penchant for big hats and American Spirit cigarettes and a nose that still bears the dent of a piercing 25 years closed." McFate's connection to HTS was prominently highlighted:

> ...the Department of Defense has started a program dubbed Cultural Operational Research Human Terrain System—based on an essay McFate co-

authored in 2005—to embed five-member teams of experienced military officers and civilian social scientists with operating brigades: an anthropological brain transplant... Heading the program is Steve Fondacaro, a Fresno native and self-described radical who retired from the Army as a colonel after 30 years in the infantry and special operations.

Several months later, the *Christian Science Monitor* ran a front-page story featuring the first HTT. It began by describing a "uniformed anthropologist toting a gun in the mountains of eastern Afghanistan." According to the obsequious report, the HTTs are akin to "a 'graduate-level counterinsurgency' unit... [created] to fine-tune aid and to undermine the intimidating grip of militants in the region." HTS was portrayed more as an intellectually informed humanitarian mission than counterinsurgency initiative; in fact, a plan to help widows market blankets and textiles was highlighted as an illustration of the HTT approach. The one-sided article included not a single criticism of the program, not a single question about the fact that the HTT cultural analyst declined to reveal her name, not a single question about the ethical compromises and contradictions inherent in such work.

The trickle of articles grew to a flood following publication (in October 2007) of a *New York Times* front-page story profiling HTS. The lead photograph was visually arresting, featuring two wide-eyed Afghan boys with a handful of uniformed US troops. The caption read: "An Afghan boy at a medical clinic set up by American Army medics and an anthropologist in the Shabak Valley in Afghanistan." The article described the HTTs as helping combat brigades "understand subtle points of tribal relations," noting that Colonel Martin Schweitzer of the US Army's 82nd Airborne Division attributed a 60 percent decrease in his unit's combat operations to the social scientists' arrival. Like the *Christian Science Monitor* piece, this one profiled a job training program for widows and gave a positive spin to HTS:

> American officers lavishly praised the anthropology program, saying that the scientists' advice has proved to be "brilliant," helping them see the situation from an Afghan perspective and allowing them to cut back on combat operations. The aim, they say, is to improve the performance of local government officials, persuade tribesmen to join the police, ease poverty and protect villagers from the Taliban and criminals.

The overall message was clear: embedded social scientists were counterinsurgency wizards who possessed the winning formula for the "war on terror."

These articles were followed by dozens more in periodicals ranging from *US News & World Report* to the *Lawrence Journal-World* (Kansas)—nearly all singing the praises of HTS. CNN anchorman Tom Foreman conducted a friendly interview with Montgomery McFate about HTS on the program *This Week at War*, without asking any critical questions. At about the same time, various radio shows (mostly affiliated with National Public Radio) broadcast stories about HTS while giving little time for critics to speak out against the program or even to ask questions. In one case, two military men, a sympathetic *New York Times* reporter, and Montgomery McFate all spoke before David Price (a critic of the program) was allowed to comment. In late 2007, PBS talk show host Charlie Rose gave McFate the red carpet treatment, ending his gushing interview with the question: "How come you're so smart?"

The sycophantic Rose also failed to ask how someone like McFate (who is not fluent in Arabic, Farsi, Urdu, or any other languages widely spoken in Iraq and Afghanistan, and had not conducted prior anthropological research in the Middle East or Central Asia) could be assigned the position of Pentagon senior social science advisor, charged with counseling the agency on HTS. Indeed, many anthropologists and ethnographers have conducted decades of research in Iraq and Afghanistan, and know much more about these regions than the social scientists currently involved in HTS. For example, Elizabeth Fernea (author of the book *Guests of the Sheik*, a sensitive and revealing description of life in a Shia village) has conducted research over nearly a half-century in Iraq. So too has her husband Robert Fernea, author of *Shaykh and Effendi*, a groundbreaking book about changing patterns of authority in southern Iraq. Barbara Nimri Aziz's book *Swimming Up the Tigris* gives a human face to Iraqis in the period following the US-led embargo, which led to the deaths of hundreds of thousands of civilians. Likewise, many anthropologists have written extensively about Afghan society. Among them is Ashraf Ghani, who has penned dozens of articles and has most recently co-written the book *Fixing Failed States*, based in part on his experience as finance minister in post-Taliban Afghanistan.

When the media fail to ask critical questions, they surrender their roles as watchdogs in a democratic society. The same media outlets mentioned above failed to question the Bush administration when it falsely asserted that Saddam Hussein had attempted to obtain "yellowcake" uranium from Africa, or that Iraq had obtained aluminum tubes for enriching uranium. Given these experiences, why should we uncritically accept media reports about a kinder, gentler counterinsurgency war in Iraq or Afghanistan—when the reports are based on nothing more than selected Pentagon sources?

A few journalists did make an effort to examine multiple sides of the story. Among them was Bryan Bender of the *Boston Globe*, who included the voices of HTS critics, and outlined the ethical dilemmas that the program might present:

> At issue is a longstanding code of ethics for the discipline, one which decrees that anthropological research should never be used to inflict harm, must always have the consent of the population being studied, and must not be conducted in secret.

Kambiz Fattahi of BBC News discussed the criticisms of the Network of Concerned Anthropologists in an article entitled "US Army Enlists Anthropologists," and gave comparable space to both supporters and critics of HTS. Fattahi noted that "very few anthropologists in the US are willing to wear a uniform and receive the mandatory weapons training," and that "many anthropologists in the US consider it unethical to work with the HTS teams [because] they are worried about the potential risks to the human subjects of their studies." In a similar vein, Ken Steir of *Time* magazine highlighted the ethical dilemmas of HTS by quoting a civilian anthropologist working for the military: "You are trying to be loyal to two communities—your subjects, and to the brigade you are attached to. It puts you in an impossible situation." The Canadian Broadcasting Corporation, BBC Radio, and the NPR program *Here and Now* also balanced differing points of view and included critical voices, but in general such reports were few and far between. The tidal wave of pro-HTS news coverage resembled a Mighty Wurlitzer, in the fashion of CIA and Pentagon Cold War propaganda.

The deluge of pro-HTS stories were the result of a concerted public relations campaign conducted by seasoned professionals. Among the HTS staff is Laurie Adler, whose official title is Strategic Communications Advisor to the Human Terrain System. Adler is best known for her work with the Lincoln Group, a "strategic communications" company that planted propaganda stories in the Iraqi press in 2005. The Pentagon contracted the company to pay Iraqi reporters from $200 to $900 monthly for writing pro-US articles for local newspapers—a "good news initiative" that Adler lamely defended at a press conference by saying: "We counter the lies, intimidation, and pure evil of terror with factual stories that highlight the heroism and sacrifice of the Iraqi people and their struggle for freedom and security." The *New York Observer* referred to the bought Iraqi journalists as "Ms. Adler's Ministry of Information," a fair charge given the overwhelming evidence. One can only wonder whether Adler is using "strategic communications" tactics similar to those employed by the Lincoln Group in Iraq to promote HTS.

Conflicting Accounts

It is appealing to think that anthropological perspectives and an appreciation of different world views might benefit everyone, from generals and prime ministers to gas station attendants and construction workers. This is perhaps the most seductive aspect of HTS that comes across in news reports—who could be against such an initiative? What is missing from such accounts is a careful review of evidence, which reveals that from the beginning, the program was designed to provide brigade commanders with intelligence for achieving short-term combat goals in a theater of war—not for improving the well-being of people living under military occupation. Collecting battlefield intelligence, increasing combat power, waging psychological warfare, co-opting local leaders: historically, these have been the uses of wartime anthropology and there is no indication that HTS is any different. Cultural awareness per se may indeed be a good thing, but not when placed in the context of counterinsurgency warfare.

HTS's supporters have discussed aspects of the program in ways that do not square with military journals, job announcements, and journalists' accounts. For example, the *Christian Science Monitor* and *The New York Times* profiled an embedded anthropologist in Afghanistan identified only by the pseudonym "Tracy." When asked by a radio show host, McFate denied that HTT analysts conceal their identities, yet a few minutes later, an embedded journalist contradicted this claim by noting, "I don't think she ['Tracy'] gave her full name" to Afghans.

HTS boosters have also stated that "espionage involves either something covert or clandestine, and this program [HTS] is neither of those things." And again: "When the Human Terrain Teams interact with indigenous populations, they're not conducting covert nor clandestine activities." Yet their work is not transparent: a deputy director of HTS, Colonel James K. Greer, claims that

> when a brigade plans and executes its operations, that planning and execution is, from an operational standpoint, classified. And so your ability to talk about it, or write an article about it, is restricted in certain ways.

Another example illustrates the slippery nature of the program. When confronted with the question of whether or not HTT personnel collect intelligence, McFate answered:

> Military intelligence traditionally is focused on the identification of enemies, whether that's a person, place, or thing... Military intelligence is generally geared towards targeting. What we're doing is not intelligence in that sense at all. It's information about the local culture and society.

However, in its 2008 *Global War on Terror Amendment*, the Department of Defense includes HTTs in precisely this category (military intelligence), alongside "Counter-intelligence teams" and "All Source Analysis":

> Additional funds are requested for All Source Analysis, Human Terrain Teams, and Counter-intelligence teams, which have proven invaluable in iden-

tifying and tracking threats. Funds requested would procure additional communications, sensors, and related equipment for deployed teams. Funding for all-source-analysis equipment will enable the integration of intelligence data from multiple sources to be combined to produce a complete operational picture.

The plan fits well with the vision of Assistant Deputy Undersecretary of Defense John Wilcox, who has a clear sense of how "human terrain" information might be used for targeting. He sent me the following email in December 2007:

> We, in the Dept of Defense, are in the business of finding, fixing, targeting the enemy and assessing afterwards how we did. The GWOT [Global War on Terror] now has an enemy that has no national boundaries, for the most case, and hides in, and amongst, friendly populations. They "terrorize" these populations to enable their hiding and surviving amongst them... Mapping the Human Terrain helps us understand, culturally and in many other areas, what the important elements are to know in order to identify the bad people (terrorists).

HTS participants have sometimes demonstrated extraordinary naivete. Take Marcus Griffin, an anthropologist embedded with a brigade in Baghdad. Griffin appears to be blissfully unaware of the possible misuses of the data he collects. On his blog, he notes:

> I've yet to be asked for targeting information there are personnel [who] are far more skilled at figuring out who stone cold killers are on the streets in need of apprehension than I will ever be. There is no need

to compromise professional ethics by engaging in targeting.

Griffin fails to acknowledge that ethical obligations extend beyond refusing to provide targeting information upon request. In a war zone, embedded social scientists may find Special Forces or CIA agents using their data to capture or kill suspects (see Chapter 3).

Human Terrain: The Very Idea

Given the fact that little official information about HTS exists, the following chapters will explore various facets of the program in order to reach a deeper understanding of its origins. Because many program details remain inaccessible to the general public, it is a partial account. Nonetheless, because of the program's high profile, the international attention that has been showered upon it, and its sheer magnitude (at nearly $200 million, this may be the biggest social science-based project in history), a critical analysis of the program is needed. The tragic deaths of two HTT members who were graduate students in political science—Michael Bhatia (killed in a May 2008 roadside bomb attack in Afghanistan) and Nicole Suveges (killed in a June 2008 bomb attack in Iraq)—further underscore the high cost of the experimental program, and the need for a better understanding of its genesis and development.

To this end, I have relied upon a range of sources. Several military journals (*Military Review*, *Parameters*, *Joint Force Quarterly*, and others) and field manuals (including the US Army's *FM 3-24: Counter-*

insurgency) were important sources of information about HTS as well as the changing nature of counterinsurgency strategy in the US armed forces. Project proposal requests and budget justification documents from the Department of Defense and the Office of the Secretary of Defense revealed much about the planned uses of human terrain data and hardware. Annual reports and newsletters from military contract firms (such as the Aptima Corporation) and federally funded research centers (such as the MITRE Corporation) also provided insight. Job descriptions for HTS positions gave a partial picture of the responsibilities of HTT members as well as the skills that they are expected to possess.

Current and former HTS employees were perhaps the most important source of information about the program. Although HTS's directors (including director Steve Fondacaro and deputy director James Greer) did not respond to my requests for information, radio interview transcripts and newspaper articles profiling HTS employees became valuable secondary sources. I have maintained direct communication via telephone and email with three former HTS employees who have become critics of the program. I contacted two of these people; the other sought me out after being forced to return early from a deployment to Iraq.

The very idea of human terrain is part and parcel of a much greater malady afflicting our society— an unrestrained "military-industrial complex" that President Dwight D. Eisenhower warned the American public about in his 1961 farewell speech. He was outraged about the poisoning of American democracy by a powerful alliance between the Pentagon and the many corporations benefiting from war. For years,

Eisenhower was also disturbed by the fact that warfare is a costly and wasteful business, robbing money from schools, hospitals, and other urgent social needs: "Every gun that is made, every warship launched, every rocket fired signifies, in the final sense, a theft from those who hunger and are not fed, those who are cold and not clothed," he noted in 1953. Perhaps the only significant difference between the Eisenhower era and the present is the fact that military contract firms—Blackwater, Halliburton, BAE Systems, and hundreds more—are ever more deeply entrenched in our country's economic and political systems. They have taken over nearly all of the functions previously carried out by our soldiers abroad, and in the process maligned our military with their corrupt practices.

In short, the military-industrial alliance was and is profoundly dehumanizing because it sacrifices human well-being and democratic values for pecuniary purposes. As we trace the trajectory of "human terrain" and HTS, we should remember that in spite of the humanistic rhetoric of its architects and supporters, in spite of the media's fawning reports about a "gentler" counterinsurgency, and in spite of the social science expertise that informs it, at the end of the day the Human Terrain System is but another wasteful and dangerous product of a military-industrial complex run amok.

Chapter 2
The Origins of Human Terrain

> In our time, political speech and writing are largely
> the defense of the indefensible.
> —George Orwell,
> "Politics and the English Language" (1946)

When I first heard the term "human terrain," a night-marish vision came to mind. I imagined a Picassoesque wasteland littered with distorted faces and distended bodies, stamped with the indelible traces of boot prints. The words are a prime example of political speech designed to defend the indefensible; indeed, "human terrain team" was declared the most euphemistic term of 2007 by the American Dialect Society. The terrible phrase has become wildly popular within certain circles in the US military establishment. But what does it mean? Where did it come from?

In an article for *Military Review* that has become the definitive statement on HTS, historian Jacob Kipp and colleagues define human terrain as

> the social, ethnographic, cultural, economic, and political elements of the people among whom a force is operating... the human population and society in the operational environment (area of operations) as defined and characterized by sociocultural, anthropologic, and ethnographic data.

Human terrain is often contrasted with geophysical terrain—a familiar concept for senior US military officials trained for conventional warfare against the Soviet Union. It implies that 21st century warriors will fight not only on a geographic plane, but also on a sociocultural plane. Some have called this "population-centric" or "culture-centric" warfare—the key to successful war fighting is the control of people. In the words of Major General Robert Scales:

> During the present "cultural" phase of the war [on terror]... intimate knowledge of the enemy's motivation, intent, will, tactical method, and cultural environment has proven to be far more important for success than the deployment of smart bombs, unmanned aircraft and expansive bandwidth.

This is more than a "hearts-and-minds" approach, for the emphasis lies primarily on recognizing and exploiting "tribal," political, religious and psychological dynamics. Montgomery McFate has noted that

> in Iraq, US and coalition forces must recognize and exploit the underlying tribal structure of the country; the power wielded by traditional authority figures; the use of Islam as a political ideology; the competing interests of the Shia, the Sunni, and the Kurds; the psychological effects of totalitarianism; and the divide between urban and rural.

Human terrain means not only identifying or manufacturing social differences, but a willingness to manipulate them as well, to attack indigenous practices of co-existence and mutual respect if necessary. In other words, to use the old colonial tactic of divide-and-conquer.

The Language of Human Terrain

Before examining the genesis of human terrain, it is worth looking at it from a linguistic point of view. For years, anthropologists and linguists have used the Sapir-Whorf hypothesis to better understand how the words we use shape the world in which we live. It postulates that language influences the thought—and consequently actions—of its users. In the case of "human terrain," linguists familiar with the Sapir-Whorf hypothesis might suggest that the term itself will tend to have objectifying and dehumanizing effects.

Consider the words of US Army Lieutenant Colonel Edward Villacres, who leads an HTT in Iraq. In a 2007 radio interview, Villacres stated that his team's objective is to

> help the brigade leadership understand the human dimension of the environment that they are working in, just like a map analyst would try to help them understand the bridges, and the rivers, and things like that. So it's an attempt to leverage the social science specialties that my team has for the benefit of the brigade.

The unusual juxtaposition of Villacres' words portrays people as geographic space to be conquered—human beings as territory to be captured, as flesh-and-blood *terra nullius* or vacant lands. Much more serious is the way the term (like "collateral damage" and "enhanced interrogation") vividly illustrates George Orwell's notion of "political language [that] is designed to make lies sound truthful and murder respectable."

"Guerrilla Warfare" and Domestic Counterinsurgency

Human terrain is not a recent concept. Although one could go back centuries to find similar metaphors, its contemporary roots stretch back 40 years, when it appeared in a report by the infamous US House Un-American Activities Committee (HUAC) about the perceived threat of the Black Panthers and other militant groups. The report's menacing title, *Guerrilla Warfare Advocates in the United States*, conjured up images of a nation under severe threat from within. From the beginning, human terrain was linked to population control:

> Traditional guerrilla warfare... [is] carried out by irregular forces, which just about always dispose of inferior weapons and logistical support in general, but which possess the ability to seize and retain the initiative through a superior control of the human terrain. This control may be the result of sheer nation-wide support for the guerrillas against a colonial or other occupying power of foreign origin; it may be the result of the ability of the guerrillas to inflict reprisals upon the population; and it can be because the guerrillas promise more to the population.

In the context of the late 1960s, the implication was clear: controlling "guerrilla" insurgents would require wresting control of contested human terrain—that is, America's city dwellers—from militant activists. Particularly worrisome is the fact that human terrain was linked to domestic counterinsurgency campaigns at an extraordinarily dark moment in US history, when the FBI's Counter-intelligence Program (COINTEL-PRO)—which repressed political dissent within the country—was in full gear.

Human terrain appeared again four years later in a book entitled *The War for the Cities* by Robert Moss, a right-wing journalist who in the 1970s edited *Foreign Report*, a journal affiliated with *The Economist* magazine. It specialized in spreading sensational rumors from intelligence agencies. At least one of Moss's books was funded by the CIA as part of a pro-Pinochet propaganda effort in the early 1970s.

Like HUAC, Moss examined the threat of diverse "urban guerrillas" including the Black Panthers,

Figure 3. The "human terrain" concept was developed in the late 1960s by the US House Un-American Activities Committee in a study of domestic counterinsurgency. HUAC hoped to defuse militant groups such as the Black Panther Party. (Photo courtesy of the US Library of Congress.)

Students for Democratic Society, and Latin American revolutionaries. Human terrain appeared in reference to the latter:

> [T]he failure of the rural guerrillas to enlist large-scale peasant backing in most areas also showed up in their distorted view of the political potential of the peasantry and their failure to study the human terrain... Che Guevara's ill-conceived Bolivian campaign was the supreme example of these deficiencies.

It is not clear whether these early uses of the human terrain concept were in some way related to one another. Nor is it clear that a straight line connects either HUAC or Moss's work to that of 21st century military analysts. But they do indicate that in at least some circles, the idea of human terrain was in motion by the 1960s. They also illustrate how from the beginning, human terrain was intimately connected with counterinsurgency.

Human Terrain at the Turn of the 21st Century

Contemporary human terrain studies date back eight years, when retired US Army Lieutenant Colonel Ralph Peters published an influential article entitled "The Human Terrain of Urban Operations." Peters is widely known as a neoconservative pundit who contributes regular columns to the *New York Post*.

Peters' ideas are as extremely reactionary as any produced by Paul Wolfowitz, Richard Perle, Douglas Feith, or others associated with the Project for the New

American Century (PNAC)—a think-tank supporting ever greater US militarization, dominance over the world's regions, and Zionist expansionism. (Many, if not most of those affiliated with PNAC are hard-boiled supporters of Israel's illegal occupation of the Palestinian territories and their continuing settlement.) For example, in 2006 Peters suggested that the US radically redraw the borders of the Middle East: Iraq would be partitioned into an "Arab Shia State," "Sunni Iraq," and "Free Kurdistan" (the latter of which would include eastern Turkey); a "Free Baluchistan" would be carved out of southeastern Iran and southwestern Pakistan; Afghanistan would absorb much of northwestern Pakistan; and nearly half of Saudi Arabia's territory would be distributed to Yemen, "Greater Jordan," and an "Islamic Sacred State" encompassing the lands between Medina and Mecca. After reading such a proposal, one cannot help but wonder what is more horrifying: the bloodshed and suffering that would be entailed by a social engineering project of this magnitude, or the equanimity with which Peters describes it. The implication is that the US government has the absolute right to partition people, land, and natural resources as it sees fit—consequences be damned.

For years, Peters has espoused a bloody version of political scientist Samuel P. Huntington's "clash of civilizations" thesis—the idea that in the post-Cold War era, conflict is most likely to occur along different cultural fault lines (for example, between "Western" and "Islamic" cultures, or between "Confucian" and "Japanese" civilizations). Peters has argued that the US military will have to inflict "a fair amount of killing" to promote economic interests and a "cultural assault" aimed at recalcitrant populations:

There will be no peace... The de facto role of the US armed forces will be to keep the world safe for our economy and open to our cultural assault. To those ends, we will do a fair amount of killing. We are building an information-based military to do that killing. There will still be plenty of muscle power required, but much of our military art will consist in knowing more about the enemy than he knows about himself, manipulating data for effectiveness and efficiency, and denying similar advantages to our opponents.

Peters has also argued that it is the "human architecture" of a city, its "human terrain... the people, armed and dangerous, watching for exploitable opportunities, or begging to be protected, who will determine the success or failure of the intervention." He describes a typology of cities ("hierarchical," "multicultural," and "tribal") and the challenges that each present to military forces: "the center of gravity in urban operations is never a presidential palace or a television studio or a bridge or a barracks. It is always human."

As Peters' ideas began circulating among military analysts, others gradually adopted human terrain. In 2001, *Army Magazine* published an article by US Army Colonel Michael Kershner that discussed Special Forces (Green Berets, Navy SEALS, etc.) training in "unconventional warfare" including "guerrilla warfare and other direct offensive, low visibility covert or clandestine operations." Kershner strongly emphasized the advantages of such an approach, particularly in the area of human terrain:

By employing indigenous troops, guerrillas or coalition forces, Special Forces can complement U.S.

conventional forces in many ways. For instance, in addition to providing fighting units for operations and security, surrogates can give us the inimitable home-court advantage: They can address the problems of the local populace, and they are familiar with the physical and human terrain... Special Forces' employment of guerrilla forces can allow us to disrupt the enemy's lines of communication and spread havoc and disorder in those areas he believes to be secure, forcing him to divert combat forces to protect them.

Two years later, in 2003, a news story on the problem of "friendly fire" appeared, in which a retired naval commander used the term:

Modern war seldom involves "front lines" any more. Instead, fights take place in a violent, confusing swirl of friends and foes... in settings that include opponents indistinguishable from civilians. "The flaw here is our lack of intimate understanding of the human terrain," says Larry Seaquist, retired Navy warship commander and Pentagon strategist. "While the American military is touting their 'total situational awareness' conferred by advanced sensors, we still have only a very hazy understanding of the human realities."

Slowly but surely, the term had crept into the military's lexicon—and eventually, ours.

Joining the Military Mainstream

By 2004, the military had mainstreamed human terrain. US Army field manual *FMI 3-07.22 Counterinsurgency Operations*, included the term in a chapter entitled "Intelligence":

> The successful conduct of counterinsurgency operations relies on the willing support and cooperation of the populations directly involved. Greater priority and awareness is needed to understand the motivations of the parties involved in the conflict and the population as a whole... This requires a detailed understanding of the cultural environment and the human terrain in which the US forces will be operating and thereby places a heavy reliance on the use of HUMINT [human intelligence].

According to the manual, the "AO [area of operations] during counterinsurgency operations includes three primary components: physical terrain and weather, society (socio-cultural, often referred to as the human terrain), and infrastructure." Furthermore,

> insurgents move among the local population the way conventional forces move over terrain. The military aspects of terrain... may be used to analyze how insurgents might use this "human terrain" to accomplish their objectives.

This was foreshadowed as early as 1992 in another military manual, *FM 7-98 Operations in Low-Intensity Conflict*:

> The population is the "key terrain" in LIC [low-intensity conflict]. It can provide both support and

security to the enemy and can represent the only terrain feature that must be seized, controlled, or defended. With the proper data base and collection effort, the S2 [intelligence officer] can begin classifying the population in the battlefield area into logical groups (tribal, religious, ethnic, political, and so forth). Their affinities, loyalties, and susceptibilities to enemy and friendly propaganda can be evaluated, graphically portrayed, maintained, and updated using the population status overlay.

By 2005, there was an avalanche of interest in "human terrain" topics. Lieutenant Colonel Michael Morris noted that the "purpose of [Al Qaeda's] covert infrastructure is to operationalize control of human terrain." Morris' use of the term "infrastructure" was synonymous with "shadow government"—in the same way that the architects of the Phoenix Program referred to the Viet Cong "infrastructure" (the civilians whom they sought to destroy).

Culture's Key Vulnerabilities: On Mohammad and Jesus Christ (but not Moses)

As Morris was articulating these ideas, Major O. Kent Strader of the US Army Command and General Staff College at Fort Leavenworth, Kansas advocated using human terrain to exploit cultural weaknesses:

Human terrain is best depicted using a systems approach... maps can depict human terrain, but their flat, non-descript nature limits their use [a]s opposed to a systems approach which depicts critical links, nodes, and key vulnerabilities within a given culture.

What might some of these key vulnerabilities be? Strader offered enticing examples from different religious traditions including Islam, Hinduism, Buddhism, and Christianity (though interestingly, Judaism was excluded):

> For instance, Najaf Imam Ali Mosque and the cities [*sic*] Shiite cemetery hold extraordinary cultural/ religious significan[ce] to Iraq's Shiites. The same could be said for Mecca's Holy Mosque or Madinah's Prophets Mosque, the Hindu temples in Varansi, Rome's Vatican or Buddhist holy sites at Lumbini, Kusinari, Isipatana, or Buddha Gaya. Cognitive cultural COGs [centers of gravity] might include desecration of the image of the Prophet

Figure 4. In a discussion of the uses of "human terrain," US Army Major O. Kent Strader notes that the Vatican and the Holy Mosque at Mecca are "cultural centers of gravity" where "culture has the potential to be weaponized." (Photos courtesy of Flickr user enggul via Creative Commons and the US Library of Congress.)

Mohammad, Jesus, Ali and/or Hussein. It should be understood not every situation has a cultural center of gravity; however, those that do should receive appropriate attention.

Just as disturbing as Strader's ideas about desecrating images of Mohammad and Jesus Christ was his conclusion, which revealed much about his final vision for using human terrain:

> the potential exists to leverage culture to coerce or preempt... In other words, culture has the potential to be weaponized. What does it mean to weaponize culture? To weaponize is to make into or use as a weapon or a potential weapon. Weaponizing culture is employing culture as an instrument of attack or defense in warfare. To operationally weaponize culture, planners must discover using cultural competence the levers or tensions within a culture than can be manipulated.

To meet this goal he recommended "developing culturally competent subject matter experts within the staff," investing in "carefully vetted cultural intelligence capital, language training, and specialized education," and introducing a program within the joint force command "to instruct leaders and key staff members how to identify cultural leverage points." (As we shall see in the next chapter, these are precisely the functions that HTS is carrying out today.)

Soon, officers and even some social scientists proposed new uses for the concept. Human terrain had become not only an entrenched ideology, but a growth industry as well, a potentially lucrative concept that might open the door to DoD funding projects with the right entrepreneurial skills. Montgomery McFate and Andrea Jackson proposed the creation of "Human Terrain" teams (more on this in the following chapter). Lieutenant Colonel Richard McConnell and colleagues suggested that US "military transition teams" training Iraqi troops employ a better understanding of human terrain: "you are not here to make this into an American unit—you are here to help this unit become the best Iraqi unit it can be." Lieutenant Colonel Fred Renzi made the case for "ethnographic intelligence" to help understand "terra incognita... the terra in this case is the human terrain."

The Defense Science Board, an influential group of scientists that advises the Office of the Secretary of Defense, highlighted "human terrain preparation" and "mapping the 'human terrain'" at the top of its list of "21st Century Strategic Technology Vectors" in 2006. The Board, which has existed for more than 50 years, consists almost entirely of members from the Pentagon, federally funded research and development corporations, and private military contract firms. They note that preparation of human terrain "will enable US forces to better understand how individuals, groups, societies, and nations behave, and then use this information to (1) improve the performance of US forces and (2) understand and shape behaviors of others in pre-, intra-, and post-conflict situations."

Among the most creative uses for "human terrain" was a training program in which the US Army National Training Center (NTC) created several mock villages at Fort Irwin, California—complete with resident Iraqi-Americans paid $4000 each for 28 days of work, according to Robert Cone in *Military Review*:

Training units in non-kinetic operations requires establishing an environment in which human terrain predominates... [U]nits can employ non-kinetic resources such as civil affairs (CA) and psychological operations (PSYOP) teams and public affairs officers; and they can conduct leader engagements, disburse money, and participate in reconstruction. To provide the human terrain necessary to train non-kinetic operations, the NTC populates its towns and villages with up to 1600 role players, of which 250 are Iraqi-Americans who remain in their roles and live in the field for the entire 14-day training event... The human element also allows the training unit to employ CA and PSYOP teams throughout its area of operations to influence the role players.

Figure 5. US military personnel search "villagers" in Medina Jabal, a mock Iraqi town located at the National Training Center in Fort Irwin, California. Some of those participating in the wartime simulation are Iraqi-Americans reportedly paid $4000 for 28-day training exercises. (Photo courtesy of Flickr user david_axe via Creative Commons.)

Human terrain has thus come to include simulated societies in a virtual post-Saddam Iraq. The mock exercises are, in essence, a dress rehearsal for an occupation.

Beyond the Pentagon

The human terrain concept began to take hold outside of the military. For example, some CIA agents appropriated the term. Henry Crumpton, leader of the CIA's Afghan campaign post-9/11, described agents working there during that period, including one

> who spoke Farsi/Dari, [and] was a cultural anthropologist intimately familiar with the tribes of the region... These CIA officers needed to map the human terrain of their patch in Afghanistan, while understanding and contributing to the larger strategy.

Pundits, politicians, and think tanks also embraced human terrain with enthusiasm. Neoconservative columnist Max Boot wrote a commentary entitled "Navigating the 'Human Terrain'," in which he referred to the need for "Americans who are familiar with foreign languages and cultures and proficient in such disciplines as intelligence collection and interrogation."

John McCain has taken a special interest in human terrain. In a September 2007 speech, he proclaimed:

> We must strive to enhance our understanding of foreign cultures—the human terrain on which we fight. We need to launch a crash program in both

civilian and military schools to increase the number of experts in strategic languages such as Arabic and Pashto.

He then suggested that social scientists be used as undercover intelligence agents:

> I would also set up a new civil-military agency patterned after the Office of Strategic Services in World War II. A modern-day OSS could draw together unconventional warfare, civil-affairs, paramilitary and psychological-warfare specialists from the military together with covert-action operators from our intelligence agencies and experts in anthropology, advertising, foreign cultures, and numerous other disciplines... It could take risks that our bureaucracies today are afraid to take—risks such as infiltrating agents who lack diplomatic cover into terrorist organizations... A cadre of such undercover operatives would allow us to gain the intelligence on terrorist activities that we don't get today.

For nearly 50 years, analysts from the RAND Corporation—a federally funded research institute—have conducted research on counterinsurgency, often with funding from the US Defense Department's Advanced Research Projects Agency (ARPA). An early example of such research occurred shortly after the arrival of American combat troops in Vietnam, when RAND sponsored a conference entitled, "Counterinsurgency: A Symposium, April 16-20, 1962." It included well-known counterinsurgency specialists such as David Galula, Anthony Jeapes, Frank Kitson, Edward Landsdale, and archaeologist Charles Bohannan. For the next decade, many debates over competing counterinsurgency theories took place at the corporation.

Throughout the 1960s, many RAND analysts embraced a rational-choice model in their approach to foreign policy. As the Vietnam War unfolded, RAND produced dozens of reports addressing various aspects of the conflict. In many cases, they offered theories that seemed to legitimate what was already occurring in the war, while at the same time shielding policy-makers from harsh realities on the ground. This changed when RAND analysts Daniel Ellsberg and Anthony Russo photocopied and leaked to the press a top-secret report, *A History of Decision-Making in Vietnam, 1945-1968*—the so-called "Pentagon Papers." The documents revealed a US government pattern of deceiving the American public about its Vietnam policies.

More recently, RAND analysts have prepared two monographs for the Office of the Secretary of Defense, both of which explicitly mention human terrain's importance in counterinsurgency. The 2007 report *Byting Back* explores the need for the Pentagon to create an information network for counterinsurgency operations, specifically a "registry-census," a "national wiki," and an expansion of cell phone usage (in order to facilitate monitoring and tracking). The first chapter notes that:

> If winning war requires understanding the terrain, winning counterinsurgency requires understanding the human terrain: the population, from its top-level political structure to the individual citizen. A thorough and current understanding of individuals and their community can help rally support of the

government [under insurgent threat] by allowing the government to meet the needs of the local population.

Another RAND report, *Heads We Win*, examines the "cognitive side of counterinsurgency" and features the following statement on its opening page: "We need the education, the insight, and the appreciation of the human terrain to develop COIN [counterinsurgency] campaigns." The monograph examines "the mind as central front" in the struggle against the "Salafist jihad" of which al-Qaeda is a part:

> Intelligence should be acquired by both "hunting" and "gathering" and should include direct and active personal observation. The government has acknowledged that there is no substitute for human intelligence (HUMINT) and that more is needed.

By 2008, human terrain had gone international and corporate at the same time. At the 3rd Global Summit on "Security for Critical Infrastructure," held at the luxurious Café Royal in the heart of London's West End, Williams Kananagha of the oil company Elf Nigeria delivered a presentation recommending that investors "study the human terrain in Nigeria and examine proactive measures to prevent incidents such as kidnapping and facility attacks" on oil rigs and refineries. At the same summit, Simon Bergman, founder of the security company Information Operations, enticed participants by suggesting how to

> improve your security strategy by mapping and influencing the human terrain in the country of

operation... develop an understanding of the human terrain and how human factors impact on security issues in critical environments in terms of culture, communications and increased security deliverables.

Human terrain was no longer relegated to back room planning at Fort Leavenworth, Kansas or the halls of the Army War College. It had truly hit the big time.

Chapter 3
Phoenix Rising? The Birth of HTS

> The old formula for successful counterinsurgency used to be ten troops for every guerrilla. Now the formula is ten anthropologists for each guerrilla.
> —US military specialist in Thailand
> (quoted in *The New York Times*, March 20, 1967)

How did "human terrain" become a system? The birth of HTS coincided with the US-led occupation of Iraq and continuing military operations in Afghanistan. Although an overwhelming majority of the American public supported the Iraq invasion in 2003, by the end of 2005 more than half thought it was a mistake. As this goes to press, nearly two-thirds of the American public are opposed to the Iraq war. Even many military and intelligence officials have grown desperate about mismanagement of the wars. (Some were against the Iraq invasion from the beginning.) In spring 2006, six retired generals publicly called for Defense Secretary Donald Rumsfeld's resignation. US casualties were mounting, Iraqi resistance groups were strengthening, and Taliban fighters were regrouping.

For years, some Pentagon officials began looking desperately for new strategies, and a renewed emphasis on counterinsurgency began to emerge. An early advocate was Major General Robert Scales, who told the US House Armed Services Committee that during the present "cultural" phase of the war... intimate knowledge of the enemy's motivation, intent, will, tactical method, and cultural environment has proven to be far more important for success than the deployment of smart bombs, unmanned aircraft, and expansive bandwidth.

Furthermore, Scales suggested the US military could learn a lesson from the empires of yesteryear:

the British Army created a habit of "seconding" bright officers to various corners of the world so as to immerse them in the cultures of the Empire and to become intimate with potentates from Egypt to Malaya. Names like China [sic] Gordon and T.E. Lawrence testify to the wisdom of such a custom... At the heart of a cultural-centric approach to future war would be a cadre of global scouts, well educated, and with a penchant for languages and a comfort with strange and distant places. These soldiers should be given time to immerse themselves in a single culture... They should attend graduate schools in disciplines necessary to understand human behavior and cultural anthropology.

The "wisdom" of citing T.E. Lawrence as a model for a new "cadre of global scouts" was questionable enough (Lawrence used terror tactics as a matter of course), but this didn't prevent Scales from going even further. In a chilling article written for *Armed Forces Journal*, Scales described "World War IV"—the wars in Iraq and Afghanistan—as the "social scientists' war." He argued that unlike WW I (the "chemists' war"), WW II (the "physicists' war"), and WW III (the "information researchers' war"), WW IV would rely upon the strategic advantage supplied by social scientists: "We are in for decades of psycho-social warfare. We must begin now to harness the potential of the social sciences in a manner not dissimilar to the Manhattan Project or the Apollo Project." Furthermore, he argued that future soldiers

> must be able to go to war with enough cultural knowledge to thrive in an alien environment. Empathy will become a weapon. Soldiers must gain the ability to move comfortably among alien cultures, to establish trust and cement relationships that can be exploited in battle.

Scales also suggested that culturally adept US soldiers should create and advise surrogate "alien armies" like those forged in "Vietnam, El Salvador, and now Iraq"—a euphemistic reference to the paramilitary death squads of the Phoenix Provincial Reconnaissance Units, the Salvadoran army, and the Iraqi Interior Ministry respectively. Backed up by Scales' ringing endorsements of British imperialist strategy and US-backed mercenary and proxy armies, the political groundwork was laid for social scientists' participation in "cultural-centric" warfare.

Scales would need not wait long. In 2005, Montgomery McFate and Andrea Jackson published a pilot proposal for a Pentagon "Office of Operational Cultural Knowledge" focused on human terrain and consisting of social scientists with "strong connections to the services and combatant commands." The social scientists would provide:

1. "on-the-ground ethnographic research (inter-views and participant observation)" on the Middle East, Central Asia, etc.;

2. "predeployment and advanced cultural training... [and] computer-based training on society and culture";

3. "sociocultural studies of areas of interest (such as North Korean culture and society, Iranian military culture, and so on)";

4. "cultural advisers for planning and operations to commanders on request" and "lectures at military institutions";

5. "experimental sociocultural programs, such as the cultural preparation of the environment—a comprehensive and constantly updated database tool for use by operational commanders and planners."

Start-up costs for the first year were estimated at $6.5 million. The proposal was consistent with one of the authors' earlier suggestions: "the national security structure needs to be infused with anthropology, a discipline invented to support warfighting in the tribal zone"—a statement of dubious historical validity.

From Drawing Board to Reality

Several months later, historian Jacob Kipp along with colleagues from the US Army's Foreign Military Studies Office (FMSO) at Fort Leavenworth, Kansas outlined the "Human Terrain System," a program to better "understand the people among whom our forces operate as well as the cultural characteristics and propensities of the enemies we now fight." They noted that Captain Don Smith headed the implementation of HTS from July 2005 to August 2006, and that the program was housed in the FMSO's Training and Doctrine Command at Fort Leavenworth. According to Kipp, each "human terrain team" (HTT) would consist of the following:

- HTT leader (major or lieutenant colonel, who is also a staff college graduate)

- Cultural analyst (civilian with an MA or PhD in cultural anthropology or sociology)

- Regional studies analyst (civilian with an MA or PhD in area studies, with language fluency)

- HT research manager (military background in tactical intelligence)

- HT analyst (military background in tactical intelligence)

The mammoth European military contractor BAE Systems began posting HTS job announcements on its company web site in 2006. By late 2007, it was joined by the Wexford Group (an affiliate of the firm CACI), MTC Technologies, Alpha Ten Technologies, and NEK Advanced Securities Group. Before deployment, HTT members received military and weapons training at a site near Fort Leavenworth. Recruitment and training were contracted to BAE Systems, who also handled administrative tasks associated with HTS—including payment of HTT members. By February 2007, the first team arrived in Afghanistan, followed by five others deployed to Iraq in summer 2007 and approximately 20 more scheduled for deployment in 2008.

HTT members are subcontractors—technically, they are BAE Systems employees. The base salary of HTT social scientists is $110,000. With "add-ons" (hazard pay, etc.) the total can reach approximately $250,000. Credible accounts have noted that HTT salaries can approach $300,000 per nine-month deployment.

What motivates social scientists to participate in HTS? Though relatively few have written about their experiences, it is worth analyzing their statements to get a fuller perspective. Corporate anthropologist Mark Dawson, in a blog entry submitted days after the tragic death of Nicole Suveges, an HTS social scientist, explained how a void in his career attracted him to the program:

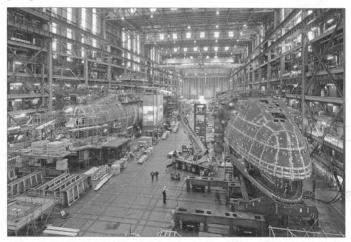

Figure 6. BAE Systems, one of the largest European military contractors, was awarded a contract for recruiting and training HTS personnel near Fort Leavenworth, Kansas. This photo was taken at the corporation's UK ship-yard at Barrow in Furness. (Photo courtesy of BAE Systems.)

I have been a corporate person for many years... Few of us have ever considered that there is a chance of getting killed during the fieldwork. So why am I doing this? God knows, the program has its warts... Its [*sic*] not the money... life would be safer (and my base pay was higher) in Silicon Valley... For me, I feel like after all my time in the corporate world, I have something to give back... Surely I can turn that skill to something more meaningful, and a longer lasting effect? So thats why I am doing it. I need to put my money where my mouth is. Do I believe in the power of cultural understanding to prevent violence or not? I do... Will this all blow up in my face? Maybe.

Archaeology professor David Matsuda joined HTS with the objective of helping end the war: "I'm a Californian. I'm a liberal. I'm a Democrat. My impetus is to come here and help end this thing," he declared in a news article. "I came here to save lives, to make friends out of enemies."

Michael Bhatia, a political scientist who became the first HTS social scientist killed in action, reportedly participated in the program because of a "need to put his studies into action." In its nationally broadcast program *All Things Considered*, National Public Radio noted that Bhatia's sister, Tricia, said that a "humanitarian ideal" attracted her brother to HTS.

Others, such as Zenia Helbig (a PhD student in religious studies) reportedly joined the program for financial reasons: *Chronicle of Higher Education* staff writer David Glenn noted that Zelbig inherited an "immigrant need for financial stability" from her Ukrainian parents. (In a phone conversation, she later told me that her parents imbued her with a sense of patriotic duty towards the country that had received them.)

Still others expressed interest in joining the program in order to "give back to [US] society." Cultural anthropologist Marcus Griffin, for example, posted the following note on his website:

> There is an obligation to give back to society in the form of new knowledge... As a professor and professional anthropologist, I have an obligation to use my skills to learn about people and to share what I learn... I've been so disappointed at the representation of anthropology on the social science sections at Barnes & Noble and Books a Million that I think a popular ethnography is in order. So I'm going to write a book about what I learn from being a part of the Human Terrain System.

Figure 7. Anthropologist Marcus Griffin is an HTS cultural analyst embedded with the 101st Airborne Division. Here he inspects a fruit stand in Ghazaliya, Iraq, January 2008. (Photo courtesy of US Department of Defense.)

These accounts reveal a variety of motivations behind social scientists' participation in the program. The question is: Are the humanitarian goals articulated by some HTT members being realized?

Since the teams have been deployed, proponents insist that HTTs "are extremely helpful in terms of giving commanders on the ground an understanding of the cultural patterns of interaction, the nuances of how to interact with those cultural groups." An enthusiastic anthropologist, Richard Shweder, has surmised that the role of the HTT social scientist is that of a "cultural translator" who gives advice to soldiers about "when not to cross their legs at meetings, how to show respect to leaders, how to arrange a party." From this perspective, HTS does little more than teach the troops cross-cultural manners. This innocuous description has been supplemented with reports from embedded journalists who assert that HTTs are involved primarily in humanitarian work, such as helping to create job training programs for widows, creating health clinics, and rebuilding mosques.

Clearly, military personnel can benefit by learning about cultural difference and cross-cultural communication, and in fact the Pentagon has provided such training (often with anthropologists' participation) long before the creation of HTS or embedded social scientists. But is this all that HTS is providing? A sober analysis of HTS work should extend beyond the accounts of embedded journalists and public relations specialists. At a minimum it should include job descriptions posted at BAE Systems and the other subcontractors tasked with recruiting anthropologists, Defense Department budget documents, and information from current and former HTT members about their work. Let us now turn to these sources.

Cross-cultural Etiquette, Humanitarian Work, or Intelligence Gathering?

Even a cursory glance at job listings for HTT personnel raises serious questions about their roles, for there are strong indications that HTS is closely connected with intelligence gathering. For example, the Wexford Group (a subsidiary of military contractor CACI) posted the following job description, dated October 24, 2007:

> The HTS project is designed to improve the gathering, interpretation, understanding, operational application and sharing of local population knowledge... the Human Terrain Analyst will serve on a unique team assisting BCT [brigade combat team] and RCT [regimental combat team] staffs in fusing cultural intelligence and information in an effective seamless process to enhance mission success... Responsibilities encompass prioritizing and categorizing requests for information, conducting near and long term analysis of the elements defining the human terrain, and assisting in planning to develop ways in which to employ other intelligence disciplines in an integrated fashion... Human Terrain Analysts apply a thorough understanding of the ops/intelligence fusion process to compile, collate, analyze and evaluate data sources and unevaluated intelligence to develop a coherent picture of the human terrain in which the BCT/RCTs operate.

The position, "Human Terrain System Cultural Analyst," requires "a Masters Degree or PhD in Cultural Anthropology, Sociology, Political Science, International Relations, or related social science fields." Another company (NEK Advanced Securities Group) advertises its HTS "Cultural Analyst" position in a way that clearly emphasizes intelligence collection experience: the position is "for Officers with CGSC [Command and General Staff College] and Brigade Staff Time as well as MI [military intelligence] experience and Warrant Officers/NCOs [non-commissioned officers] with Military Intelligence and 18F (Special Forces Intel) MOS [military occupational specialty] qualifications and experience." These descriptions bear little resemblance to the humanitarian missions described in *The New York Times*, the *Christian Science Monitor*, and other articles.

More detail is provided by Jacob Kipp and colleagues—particularly the development of a database of ethnographic and cultural information. In their outline of HTS, they discuss how HTTs will supply brigade commanders with "deliverables" including a "user-friendly ethnographic and sociocultural database of the area of operations that can provide the commander data maps showing specific ethnographic or cultural features." They note that HTTs will use Mapping Human Terrain (MAP-HT) software, "an automated database and presentation tool that allows teams to gather, store, manipulate, and provide cultural data from hundreds of categories," including "key regional personalities, social structures, links between clans and families, economic issues, public communication, agricultural production, and the like." A US-based "reachback research" center "will systematically receive information from deployed HTTs... Data will be collected, catalogued, and placed into a central database." In addition, "other US government agencies will also have access to the central database," including the CIA, an agency with a long history of covert operations that have included overseeing torture sessions, plotting coups d'etat, coordinating assassinations, and most recently creating a secret overseas prison network.

HTT member Edward Villacres' presentation at the 2007 "Director of National Intelligence Open Source Conference" gives additional insight into the links between HTS and intelligence collection. His presentation included a slide stating that

> Human Terrain Teams [are] supported by a Map-Human Terrain (MAP-HT) Toolkit, which provides the capability to store, analyze, and visualize human terrain knowledge to build and preserve an unclassified repository, which can be transferred into the DCGS [Distributed Common Ground System] architecture to ensure horizontal and vertical information sharing.

DCGS is, in layman's terms, an integrated real-time network of intelligence systems "to discover and access relevant intelligence from the military, as well as the US 'three-letter' intelligence agencies and the nation's coalition partners." In the words of Air Force Colonel Alan Tucker, who is DCGS program director,

> Our ultimate goal is to provide the ability to find and identify time-sensitive targets... Through DCGS, you will see increases in speed, in terms of intelligence collection, and in lethality, in terms of our ability to prosecute targets.

Apart from Villacres' presentation, Lieutenant Colonel David W. Morrison has noted that "MAP-HT injects into DGCS-A," referring to the Army's version of the network.

HTS director Steve Fondacaro's words fully support these descriptions. According to reporter Lindsay Beyerstein, Fondacaro "confirmed that the CIA or other intelligence agencies could access the [HTS] database, but he doesn't envision intelligence agencies as major consumers of HTT data." He told Beyerstein:

> Any government organization that has an interest [will have access to the database]. The DoD is the primary focus, but also State, the Transportation Command, any of the State Department organizations focused on provincial reconstruction. There's all this concern about intelligence, but they are just one customer of many, many customers.

Such words do little to reassure those concerned about CIA agents, Special Operations forces, or others using HTS data for "neutralizing" suspected insurgents and sympathizers.

Combat Power

Other sources emphasize the ways in which human terrain data will improve "combat power." For example, the Office of the Secretary of Defense's budget justification for 2007 bluntly describes the objective of HTS:

to reduce IED [improvised explosive device] incidents via improved situational awareness of the human terrain by using "green layer data/unclassified" information to understand key population points to win the "will and legitimacy" fights and surface the insurgent IED networks... capability must be further developed to provide a means for commanders and their supporting operations sections to collect data on human terrain, create, store, and disseminate information from this data, and use the resulting information as an element of combat power.

In unvarnished language, the OSD budget reveals that the goal of HTS data is to help "win the 'will and legitimacy' fight" (through propaganda) and to serve "as an element of combat power" (i.e. as a weapon).

HTS supporters have equivocated when asked whether data is used to target Iraqis or Afghans. In a radio interview, HTS architect Montgomery McFate stated:

The intent of the program is not to identify who the bad actors are out there. The military has an entire intelligence apparatus geared and designed to provide that information to them. That is not the information that they need from social scientists.

Yet the "intent" of the program is not the issue. The problem is how brigade commanders, DoD officials, CIA operatives, or other covert agents will use human terrain data ("as an element of combat power" and "to enhance mission success") once it is distributed widely.

In the same interview, the same HTS booster claimed that HTT social scientists have "a certain amount of discretion" with data, while providing no evidence that safeguards exist to prevent others from using it against informants. When asked about why the program lacks independent oversight, she answered: "We would like to set up a board of advisors. At the moment, however, this program is proof of concept... [I]t's not a permanent program. It's an experiment."

Phoenix Reborn?

Before examining the implications of this statement, it is worth taking a brief historical detour while recalling the full title of the article by Kipp and his colleagues: "Human Terrain System: A CORDS for the 21st Century." What if we took Kipp at his word? What if HTS took the shape of a latter-day CORDS?

As noted in Chapter 1, CORDS stands for Civil Operations and Revolutionary Development Support, a counterinsurgency program developed during the Vietnam War era by the US military in conjunction with the South Vietnamese government. Taking its cue from the colonial powers of previous centuries, the Pentagon referred to CORDS as a "pacification" initiative.

Among other things, it gave rise to the nefarious Phoenix Program (aimed at eliminating the Viet Cong "infrastructure"), a secret campaign that eventually resulted in the killing of thousands of suspected cadres. Phoenix was coordinated by the CIA and staffed by CIA mercenaries as well as US and South Vietnamese military personnel.

CORDS/Phoenix consisted of numerous elements, including an amnesty program, civil affairs programs, counterterror teams, armed propaganda units, interrogation centers, "Revolutionary Development" cadres, and the "Census Grievance" program. According to former CIA operative Tom Donohue, Census Grievance was particularly important for collecting intelligence:

> Everybody knows the government takes a census, so you'd have a guy make a map of every house in the village—put everything into perspective. Then the edict was issued that once a month every head of household had to talk to the Census Grievance officer... Basically, the census, scaled down, had three questions: (One) What would you like the GVN [government of South Vietnam] to do for you? All of the precinct-type needs. "A bridge across this

Figure 8. CORDS personnel talk to villagers from Dinh Tri hamlet, Binh Dinh province, Vietnam, September 1969. After building rapport with local leaders, CORDS personnel gathered intelligence about suspected Viet Cong cadres. (Photo courtesy of Texas Tech University Vietnam Archive.)

particular canal would save us a three-mile walk to get our produce to market." Very legitimate needs. (Two) Is there anybody in the GVN giving you a hard time? Are the police at the checkpoint charging you a toll every time you take your rutabagas to market? (Three) Is there anything you want to tell me about the Vietcong? If the answer was no, the whole thing wasn't pursued, but once a month the head of household had to touch base... If the Census Grievance officer finds that X number of people say they need a bridge... money is allocated... Census Grievance produced a good bit of intelligence.

Another former CIA operative, Nelson Brickham, noted that his group "wanted access to its [Census Grievance's] intelligence because they could get intelligence we didn't have access to... They [Vietnamese police Special Branch province chiefs] took Census Grievance stuff and turned around and used it in the counterterror teams," CIA mercenaries who were particularly brutal in the way they dealt with villagers. Census Grievance officers built rapport with local villagers, but the information they collected was in fact used more for intelligence than for winning hearts and minds.

Could HTT data be used in this way? HTT member Marcus Griffin, a cultural anthropologist, has blogged about aspects of his work, and has on several occasions made reference to census taking as a part of his responsibilities. At times it seems as if Griffin could be describing Census Grievance:

- This past Saturday, I was helping a platoon improve its means of collecting census data. In particular I was interested in improving our understanding of Internally Displaced Persons (IDPs). We need to know to what extent they are food insecure and how families are coping with the burden of taking on six or more family members.

- One example [of our work] is assessing the impact of poor essential services such as sewage, water, electricity, and trash on the population's willingness to provide aid and comfort to insurgents. Improve the quality of life of local residents by building their satisfaction with the Iraqi Government and they will likely be less willing to harbor insurgents.

- In Iraq, US Forces are conducting stability operations—doing things to build up the capacity of the Iraqi government in order for it to run itself. Anthropology contributes to this effort by helping identify who key stakeholders are, people that can get things done instead of US Forces doing it for them.

- I started interviewing an older man... I just wanted to talk about food sharing and get his thoughts on why no one in Iraq goes hungry as some people had been telling me. I said I wanted to know about this to help commanders make better decisions about ensuring essential services, particularly access to food in markets, were adequate. There was no other benefit other than that maybe.

- While [I was] interviewing a man about his views on how political parties are vying for power and helping or hurting people in various neighborhoods, his cell phone rang...

- We are trying to measure this [poverty] by getting expense diaries from a variety of people from different income levels. We look at the food ration program, how much a variety of goods cost historically and currently, and the housing situation (which is not good). The reason for this research is to better understand that segment of the population in Baghdad that are vulnerable to militia violence and coercion as well as to understand the role the Iraqi Government plays in (not) providing essential services to its people.

Like the Phoenix-era Census Grievance interviews mentioned by Tom Donohue, Griffin's interviews are geared towards determining material needs. Some interviews venture into the realm of politics and political parties (recall Donohue's description of Census Grievance questions about the Viet Cong). Under these circumstances it is difficult to imagine how an HTT social scientist could refuse a brigade commander's request for interview tapes or transcripts, given the strict military chain of command. Furthermore, once HTS data is distributed widely, what is to prevent it from being used by Special Operations forces or the CIA for targeting suspected insurgents, Ba'ath party sympathizers, or the so-called Al Qaeda "infrastructure"? What is to prevent its use for real-time targeting?

HTTs and the AAA

Out of these and other concerns, opposition to HTS from some social scientists began to coalesce by the fall of 2007. A group called the Network of Concerned

Anthropologists began circulating a "Pledge of Non-Participation in Counter-Insurgency" and within months hundreds of anthropologists and students of anthropology had signed.

Such efforts culminated in a statement from the American Anthropological Association's (AAA) Executive Board which focused on the potential harm that might be done to people being studied as HTS research subjects, difficulties that anthropologists (especially armed anthropologists) might have in obtaining voluntary informed consent from Iraqis or Afghans, and the dangers to which anthropologists might be exposed:

> the Executive Board of the American Anthropological Association concludes (i) that the HTS program creates conditions which are likely to place anthropologists in positions in which their work will be in violation of the AAA Code of Ethics and (ii) that its use of anthropologists poses a danger to both other anthropologists and persons other anthropologists study. Thus the Executive Board expresses its disapproval of the HTS program.

The Executive Board statement explicitly mentioned the context of the unilateral and illegal US-led invasion of Iraq as an important factor in its decision:

> In the context of a war that is widely recognized as a denial of human rights and based on faulty intelligence and undemocratic principles, the Executive Board sees the HTS project as a problematic application of anthropological expertise, most specifically on ethical grounds. We have grave concerns about the involvement of anthropological knowledge and

skill in the HTS project. The Executive Board views the HTS project as an unacceptable application of anthropological expertise.

At the 2007 AAA conference (held in late November and early December), a number of key panels addressed aspects of emerging links between the military and anthropologists. Some HTS staff members were sighted at the conference. For example, a former US intelligence officer (now studying anthropology) witnessed Laurie Adler, the strategic communications director for TRADOC, attending a panel presentation entitled, "Against the Weaponization of Anthropology." Adler, joined by Jessica Lawrence of the US Army, was reportedly writing down the names and institutional affiliations of scholars signing an anti-counterinsurgency pledge circulated by the Network of Concerned Anthropologists. Though Adler later claimed that she was only recording the names of fellow alumni from the University of Chicago, her actions probably had a chilling effect that discouraged others from signing the pledge.

Several social scientists involved with HTS became defensive after the AAA Executive Board issued its statement. Marcus Griffin posted several responses to his web site in response to the AAA's concerns over lack of voluntary informed consent:

> Informed consent without coercion due to the fact that research participants may be surrounded by soldiers with guns is a valid question. On the other hand, how does an anthropologist's status as a foreigner with obvious social capital working in remote rural places coerce villagers to answer questions? Isn't there some kind of coercion going on in

the very beginning? If governmental, police, and military officials clearly gave me permission to work and live in a jungle, does a subsistence farmer really feel they have much choice but to answer my questions?

Griffin's implication—that a farmer interviewed by an anthropologist with a government-issued research visa is subjected to as much coercion as a farmer "surrounded by soldiers with guns" being interviewed by an armed anthropologist—is disingenuous, to say the least. One wonders whether Griffin's Iraqi informants would agree, given his preference for sidearms. (His website includes photos in which he is posing with an M9 pistol strapped to the thigh.)

Equally as disturbing is Griffin's terse response to how HTS might pose dangers for the people being studied:

> [AAA] Ethical Concern #4: Research results may be used in the short or long term to target populations and therefore violates the rule to not harm people being studied. As stated above, this depends on the kinds of research an anthropologist conducts and the kinds of missions the US Army conducts. The concern is rooted, again, in a lack of understanding of military operations during a peace and stability mission. Explaining it is beyond the scope of this blog.

Why is such a point beyond the scope of the blog? What aspect of military operations is not understood by the AAA's Executive Board? Readers are left with the impression that either Griffin has something to hide, or that he refuses to deal with concerns regarding the safety of research participants in Iraq. His dismissive response casts a shadow over the entire discipline. So too do Griffin's boastful statements about "going native" with the military.

The Practical Utility of HTS Data

To better understand his position, I emailed Marcus Griffin with specific questions about his work, his methods, the destination of the data he was collecting, and the availability of HTT data to outside researchers. I received the following response:

> Dr. Gonzalez,
>
> I am currently doing fieldwork and consider publishing or commenting with academic-rhetorical authority premature. The interview you mention was done at my former commander's encouragement. When I am closer to the end of my deployment (August) I will have more to say and will be publishing my results. My blog is primarily for my students' benefit and should be cited with care.
>
> Sincerely,
> Marcus Griffin

Another HTT social scientist, Dave Matsuda, did not respond to multiple requests for information. Nor did HTS director Steve Fondacaro. Nor did James K. Greer, the deputy director of HTS.

Their silence was disconcerting, particularly when I considered the comments of an army commander with experience in Iraq, Lieutenant Colonel Gian Gentile. His response to Griffin's blog postings should raise red flags for those concerned about the misuse of HTS data:

> Dear Dr Griffin:
>
> Don't fool yourself. These Human Terrain Teams whether they want to acknowledge it or not, in a generalized and subtle way, do at some point contribute to the collective knowledge of a commander which allows him to target and kill the enemy in the Civil War in Iraq.
>
> I commanded an Armored Reconnaissance Squadron in West Baghdad in 2006. Although I did not have one of these HTTs assigned to me (and I certainly would have liked to) I did have a Civil Affairs Team that was led by a major who in his civilian life was an investment banker in New York City and had been in the area I operated for about 6 months prior. He knew the area well and understood the people and the culture in it; just like a HTT adviser would. I often used his knowledge to help me sort through who was the enemy and who was not and from that understanding that he contributed to I was able to target and sometimes kill the enemy. So stop sugarcoating what these teams do and end up being a part of; to deny this fact is to deny the reality of the wars in Iraq and Afghanistan.
>
> I am in favor of this program of HTTs and see great utility in it for combat commanders. I understand the debate too between these field anthropologists who are part of the HTTs and academia. I think academia is wrong to chastise these people for being a part of the HTTs. But I also think that people like you should call a spade a spade and accept the reality of the effects that these HTTs produce.
>
> —Lieutenant Colonel Gian P. Gentile

In a similar vein, University of Montana student and Iraq War veteran Matthew L. Schehl expressed concern over HTS based on his military experience. In a blog maintained by the American Anthropological Association, he noted:

I am a graduate student of social anthropology; prior to this, however, I was a US Army military intelligence non-commissioned officer... I ran a Tactical Human Intelligence Team (THT) in Central Iraq [from 2003-2005]... The HTS program is intended to sub-contract this [local] knowledge to those who are "experts" at culture. Now were this "expert opinion" intended to either contribute to the (sustainable) welfare of target populations, or provide for (vastly) improved understanding of US personnel towards this, I would be moved to endorse this program. Its intention, however, is not: guidance and information provided by anthropologists is subordinated to achieving operational ("mission") success. In my experience, this translates into at least three severe problems:

1. "Success" is defined in the short term... specific objectives are pursued without necessary regard for long-term implications (e.g., what happens if/when US troops are withdrawn?);

2. Information produced will tend toward a narrow conception of culture and social systems, i.e. that information which is only as relevant as its immediate utility to the field commander, fostering a simplified ideation of "good guy, bad guy," without regard to social or historic contexts and processes (e.g., much literature exists documenting US-supported state authorities as culpable for

structural violence, as opposed to "anti-democratic" revolutionary movements);

3. The utilization of such information is subject to the whims and spot decisions of the field commander, with or without the development of an IRB equivalent, and whether or not "in the service of human freedom."

My most immediate objection, though, is that which hits hardest home to me. A primary motivation for me to leave the US government was its systematic inability and unwillingness to enact meaningful change in Iraq... it hurt me to watch good people unnecessarily suffer and die, Americans and Iraqis. I shudder at the thought of anthropologists contributing to this.

I contacted Schehl by telephone and asked him what he thought about the possibility that HTTs are primarily involved in humanitarian work and cultural awareness training, not intelligence gathering. He responded by stating that based on his experience, such claims are bogus because military units are by nature focused upon short term goals (namely military operations that will promote the creation of a stable environment for US corporations to conduct business), not the long term well-being of Iraqis.

A more complete picture emerges once the puzzle pieces are put into place. The Pentagon is faced with crumbling public support for a war that has become a quagmire. It creates a series of new programs that appear to demonstrate how social scientists might bring a more culturally sensitive approach to warfighting, while collecting new intelligence information from

HTT "boots on the ground." Some social scientists protest, and in response the Pentagon launches a media offensive while individual HTT personnel dismiss critics of the HTS program. And as all of these factors play out, HTT data—more appropriately called intelligence—is transmitted to a common database and HTS expands dramatically in size. Given these realities, it is worth asking once again what lessons history might hold for the current situation.

Weaponizing Culture:
Local Data and Psychological Warfare

In addition to using census data for intelligence purposes, CORDS/Phoenix and its predecessors made use of cultural information as a weapon. In particular, counterterror teams and their US Special Forces counterparts used knowledge about Vietnamese religious beliefs and myths in brutal psychological warfare operations. According to Douglas Valentine, author of *The Phoenix Program*:

> The CTs [counterterror teams, i.e. CIA mercenaries] taught [US Navy SEAL Elton] Manzione and his SEAL comrades the secrets of the psywar campaign, which in practice meant exploiting the superstitions, myths, and religious beliefs of the Vietnamese. One technique was based on the Buddhist belief that a person cannot enter heaven unless his liver is intact. So Manzione would snatch an NVA [North Vietnam army] courier off the Ho Chi Minh Trail or sneak into a VCI's [Viet Cong "infrastructure"] hooch at night, crush the man's larynx, then use his dagger to remove the man's liver.

In an interview, Manzione described the way in which his team terrorized uncommitted civilians living near the demilitarized zone:

> We left our calling card nailed to the forehead of the corpses we left behind. They were playing card size with a light green skull with red eyes and red teeth dripping blood, set against a black background. We hammered them into the third eye, the pituitary gland, with our pistol butts. The third eye is the seat of consciousness for Buddhists, and this was a form of mutilation that had a powerful psychological effect.

Such accounts graphically illustrate how cultural information can be used for the most macabre purposes, in the name of counterinsurgency "psy-ops."

HTS supporters have repeatedly claimed that their objective is to "provide commanders with relevant knowledge about local societies in brigade's area of operations and assist brigade staffs in developing courses of action that emphasize the use of non-lethal tactics (e.g. negotiation, infrastructure development, and provision of medical care)." But in the current context such "relevant knowledge"—freely accessible via DCGS or some other "top-secret web" available to government agencies—can easily be used as a weapon by 21st century "counterterrorism teams" or death squads. The history of operations like CORDS/Phoenix—and the use of weaponized culture tailor-made for use against people from different ethnicities, religions, or nationalities—are fair warning to social scientists who think that they are free to set the terms of engagement with military and intelligence agencies.

As Phoenix grew in size, program personnel expanded its database to include names of hundreds of thousands of people who were to be "neutralized." By 1967, it featured a computerized database, according to Valentine:

> Phoenix was enhanced with the advent of the Viet Cong Infrastructure Information System... [In January 1967] the Combined Intelligence Staff fed the names of 3000 VCI (assembled by hand at area coverage desks) into the IBM 1401 computer at the Combined Intelligence Center's political order of battle section. At that point the era of the computerized blacklist began... VCIIS became the first of a series of computer programs designed to absolve the war effort of human error and war managers of individual responsibility.

Phoenix Program personnel collected a wealth of intelligence information, which was then passed on to "analysts." Valentine notes:

> VCIIS compiled information... on VCI boundaries, locations, structures, strengths, personalities, and activities... [it] included summary data on each recorded VCI in the following categories: name and aliases; whether or not he or she was "at large"; sex, birth date, and place of birth; area of operations; party position; source of information; arrest date; how neutralized; term of sentence; where detained; release date; and other biographical and statistical information, including photographs and fingerprints, if available... Phoenix analysts [were able] instantly to access and cross-reference data, then decide who was to be erased.

As a result, between 1967 and 1972, South Vietnamese officials, US advisors, and mercenaries "erased" more than 26,000 suspected members of the so-called Viet Cong "infrastructure," including civilians—acts that amounted to war crimes. Nowhere is this mentioned in Kipp's depiction of HTS as "a CORDS for the 21st century."

Will HTS one day be employed for such ends? The potential risk to Iraqi, Afghan, and US civilians is too great to take the question lightly. Nor is this only a remote possibility. The gross mismanagement of HTS by its directors and BAE Systems personnel (see below) could easily lead to a situation in which sensitive HTT data is appropriated by agents seeking to make use of all available intelligence information.

Lessons from the Past

If this is not reason enough for concern, consider again the description offered by Kipp and colleagues: to "ensure that any data obtained through the HTS does not become unnecessarily fettered or made inaccessible to the large numbers of Soldiers and civilians routinely involved in stability operations, the information and databases assembled by the HTS will be unclassified." In fact, Kipp states that "databases will eventually be turned over to the new governments of Iraq and Afghanistan to enable them to more fully exercise sovereignty over their territory."

Is this an appropriate use for the data? Once again, CORDS/Phoenix provides an instructive example. When given the opportunity, US-backed South

Vietnamese president Nguyen Van Thieu "us[ed] Phoenix to repress his domestic opponents." After US officials encouraged South Vietnamese officers to hunt down communist cadres, police chiefs and others used extraordinary means to give the impression that Phoenix was working—including "unjustified arrest, false accusation, and arbitrary detention" of suspects. Innocent people were frequently rounded up as the result of personal vendettas, as many enthusiastic South Vietnamese officials wanted to keep tapping into the "CIA's bottomless black bag and irrational obsession with internal security at any cost." In particular, Thieu's signing of Law 280 in 1968 allowed him to "begin persecuting domestic opponents whose 'compatible left' political organizations fell under Law 280's definition of VCI 'cadre'," according to Valentine.

This history might seem remote, but recent comments by Defense Secretary Robert Gates about CORDS and social scientists are troubling to say the least:

> However uncomfortable it may be to raise Vietnam all these years later, the history of that conflict is instructive... The CORDS program, as it was known, involved more than a thousand civilian employees from USAID and other organizations, and brought the multiple agencies into a joint effort... By the time US troops were pulled out, the CORDS program had helped pacify most of the hamlets in South Vietnam... The importance of deploying civilian expertise has been relearned—the hard way... We also have increased our effectiveness by joining with organizations and people outside the government—untapped resources with tremendous

potential. For example, in Afghanistan the military has recently brought in professional anthropologists as advisors. *The New York Times* reported on the work of one of them, who said, "I'm frequently accused of militarizing anthropology. But we're really anthropologizing the military." And it is having a very real impact.

Gates' speech provided no answers for those concerned about how the "very real impact" of a new CORDS is putting innocent Iraqis and Afghans in harm's way. It did not explain how social scientists might succeed in "anthropologizing the military" when historically, Pentagon officials have tended to use only that anthropological knowledge that helps them meet narrow objectives and disregarded the rest. Nor did it hint at the fact that many of those participating in the best-known element of CORDS, the Phoenix Program, committed war crimes.

The experiences of renowned anthropologist Gregory Bateson stand as a warning to those who might think that deeply entrenched institutions like the Defense Department or the CIA can be "anthropologized" by a handful of social scientists. During World War II, Bateson contributed to the war effort by designing and disseminating propaganda, by preparing intelligence reports for the Office of Strategic Services (the precursor to the CIA), by suggesting ways that the US might learn from the Soviet Union's conquests of its ethnic minorities, by recommending intelligence gathering in post-war India to help prop up the British colonial order, and by participating in covert operations in Burma. Yet Bateson came to regret his actions, "not because of any failures, but because of the successes in which native peoples were ill treated, manipulated, and disempowered," notes David Price in his book *Anthropological Intelligence*. As the Pentagon aggressively seeks to recruit social scientists for its newest venture, it is critical to remember the past—a past in which military and intelligence agencies enlisted anthropologists for ethically questionable practices, US forces and mercenaries manipulated, abused, and sometimes killed innocent people, and the US government misinformed its own citizens about what was occurring in theaters of war.

Postscript: HTS and Its Discontents

In late 2007, credible accounts began to emerge about difficulties plaguing HTS, including "recruitment shortfalls," "haphazard and often pointless" training, and a program "nearly paralyzed by organizational problems." Sheila Miyoshi Jager reported that Steve Fondacaro, "head of the Human Terrain project, confided recently that since the HTS' inception in 2006, he had been able to hire only a handful of anthropologists."

Former HTS employee Zenia Helbig has reported that much of the HTS staff are woefully ineffective, including the BAE Systems representative charged with coordinating the operation near Fort Leavenworth. Helbig has also noted that BAE Systems, responsible for HTT recruitment and training, is exceedingly inept and more concerned with maximizing profits than with meeting program objectives. According to Helbig, BAE Systems was awarded the

HTS contract through an omnibus provision that outsources work to preferred contractors. If true, this would fit a decades-old pattern of a privatized Pentagon characterized by mismanagement, waste, and war profiteering.

In her public criticism of the program, Helbig claimed that during four months of training, there was no discussion about the potential harm that might befall Iraqis or Afghans, and no discussion of ethical issues. Furthermore, she declared that "HTS' greatest problem is its own desperation. The program is desperate to hire anyone or anything that remotely falls into the category of 'academic,' 'social science,' 'regional expert,' or 'PhD,'" which has often resulted in the employment of grossly incompetent HTS personnel.

It is clear that BAE Systems and other contractors have resigned themselves to looking beyond anthropology for HTS. They have begun targeting students of political science and international relations for recruitment, according to sources with HTS/HTT experience. According to McFate and Fondacaro, "HTS now has a surfeit of CVs [curriculum vitaes] on file as a result of the recent publicity" afforded to it by the media. One thing is certain: notwithstanding its problems, the program's steadily increasing budget—which has reached a total of nearly $200 million for fiscal years 2006 through 2008—indicates that HTS will continue to grow for the foreseeable future.

Chapter 4
Imaginary Terrorists, Virtual Tribes:
HTS as Technological Fantasy

And then there is the precognitive dystopia famously imagined by the science fiction writer Philip K. Dick in his 1956 short story "The Minority Report"—just replace Dick's three gibbering psychics who predict future crimes with data centers full of ultrapowerful computers that do something similar, only without the gibbering.
—Harry Goldstein, "Modeling Terrorists" (2006)

Imagine a computer program that tells its users which neighborhoods in a distant city—Baghdad, Kabul, or Islamabad—are dangerous. The program predicts whether these neighborhoods are prone to riots, gun violence, sniper attacks, or bombings. It forecasts when the events are likely to occur. With all the speed and imagery of a video game the program also identifies the names of people who are likely participants in the violence, as well as their addresses, fingerprints, ID photos, relatives, friends, and associates.

Such a program might appear to be beyond the realm of possibility, but the Pentagon is spending tens of millions of dollars in a quest to find a technological holy grail that predicts "hot spots" ranging from organized protest marches to full-blown insurgent attacks. Raw data for these programs will come from "boots on the ground" collecting information on human terrain. This suggests that the human terrain concept is ripe for incorporation into a new technological fantasy world being created by the Pentagon, military contractors, and university-based research laboratories—a military-industrial-academic complex for the 21st century.

Model Terrorists and Simulated "Tribes"

Pentagon budgets reflect an increasing commitment to "cultural knowledge" acquisition. Consequently, a group of engineers, mathematicians and computer scientists are expressing acute interest in human terrain for modeling, simulation, and gaming programs. Among them is Barry Silverman, a University of Pennsylvania engineering professor who bluntly asks in a recent article: "Human Terrain Data: What Should We Do with It?"

Silverman and his team of graduate students have pioneered development of computerized behavior modeling programs designed to uncover the hidden motivations of terrorists and their networks, and they hope to integrate HTS data into these programs. *IEEE Spectrum* (an engineering journal) reports that their simulations, funded by the Pentagon's Defense Modeling and Simulation Office and the Office of Naval Research (among others) are

> an astoundingly sophisticated amalgamation of more than 100 models and theories from anthropology, psychology, and political science, combined with empirical data taken from medical and social science field research, surveys, and experiments.

The goal is to predict how terrorists, soldiers, or ordinary citizens might react to "a gun pointed in the face, a piece of chocolate offered by a soldier... [Silverman] is now simulating a small society of about 15,000 leader and follower agents organized into tribes, which squabble over resources." At the heart of Silverman's simulations are "performance moderator functions" representing

> physical stressors such as ambient temperature, hunger, and drug use; resources such as time, money, and skills; attitudes such as moral outlook, religious feelings, and political affiliations; and personality dispositions such as response to time pressure, workload, and anxiety.

Silverman makes optimistic claims about the potential utility of HTS data for human social profiling, though he has not yet obtained any of it: "the HT datasets are an invaluable resource that will permit us in the human behavior M&S [modeling and simulation] field to more realistically profile factions, and their leaders and followers."

Similarly, a Dartmouth research team has created the Laboratory for Human Terrain, "focused on the foundational science and technology for modeling, representing, inferring, and analyzing individual and organizational behaviors." It includes an engineer, a mathematician, and a computer scientist who specialize in "adversarial intent modeling, simulation, and prediction," "dynamic social network analysis," and "discovery of hidden relationships and organizations." The Pentagon awarded a $250,000 grant to team member Eugene Santos to develop a "Dynamic Adversarial Gaming Algorithm" (DAGA) for predicting how individuals or groups... react to social, cultural, political, and economic interactions... DAGA can evaluate how rhetoric from religious leaders combined with recent allied killing of radical military leaders, and perceptions of potential economic growth can cause shifts in support from moderate or radical leadership.

The Dartmouth group uses the "Adversary Intent Inferencing" (AII) model, a prototype of which was tested using scenarios replicating Gulf War battles. As of January 2008, Santos was the principal investigator to grants from US military and intelligence agencies totaling more than $3 million.

Another researcher interested in developing human terrain applications is Swen Johnson, founder and CEO of Socio-Cultural Intelligence Analysis, Inc. (SCIA), a Virginia-based company that claims to be "bringing the social sciences to the intelligence community" through "intelligence analysts specifically trained in 'human terrain' research and analysis." Their clients include the Defense Department. SCIA's website features an image of Auguste Rodin's statue "The Thinker" alongside a quip from a US Naval War College professor: "the information we desire the most about the enemy—his real fighting power and his intentions—lie in the psychological and human dimensions rather than the physical." It informs readers that Johnson has a PhD in sociology and 13 years of experience as a US Army counterintelligence agent.

In October 2007, SCIA was awarded one of five research awards from the US Geospatial Intelligence Foundation—a not-for-profit organization funded by military contractors and government intelligence agencies. According to the Foundation, Johnson has "dedicated himself to creating Human Terrain Analysis Teams across the Defense Department," while SCIA's "empirical, quantitative and group-based sociological focus have transformed traditional geospatial models of human behavior into more accurate geo-social models, bringing GEOINT to the cutting edge of intelligence analysis." It is unclear whether Johnson and SCIA are working directly with HTS personnel, analyzing HTS data, or simply using the "human terrain" label, but their work seeks to expand social science research in the service of military intelligence.

Wired magazine's blog reports a boom in wartime simulation projects, including Purdue University's Synthetic Environment for Analysis and Simulation (SEAS) which can "gobble up breaking news, census data, economic indicators, and climactic events in the real world, along with proprietary information such as military intelligence." According to *National Defense* magazine, Purdue's "Iraq and Afghanistan computer models are the most highly developed and complex. Each has about five million individual nodes that represent entities such as hospitals, mosques, pipelines, and people."

Forecasting Human Behavior

The Pentagon has already committed itself to funding similar research to the tune of $19 million over the next five years. According to a DoD "Budget Item Justification" dated February 2007, the "Human, Social and Culture Behavior Modeling" (HSCB) program is slated for development between 2008 and 2013. Since "current military operations need and future operations will demand the capability to understand the social and cultural terrain and the various dimensions of human behavior within those terrains," the research program "will develop technologies for human terrain understanding and forecasting" for "intelligence analysis," "database infrastructure," "human behavior based theory for DoD models," and "visualization infrastructure." By 2008, the program is scheduled to begin

> development of the methods and tools to allow remote and "boots on the ground" collection of pedigreed social and cultural information relating to a population (local, regional, global), including the print, voice, and video media, social networks, and cultural, religious, and tribal alliances. This work will be focused on areas operation in CENTCOM [Central Command], PACOM [Pacific Command], and EUCOM [European Command]. The work will identify methods to collect relevant socio-cultural data for Phase 0-Phase 4 operations.

(In military terms, operational "phases" include: [Phase 0] planning and coalition building; [Phase 1] combat preparation; [Phase 2] initial combat operations; [Phase 3] combat; and [Phase 4] post-combat or "stability" operations.)

As far as HSCB is concerned, the name of the game is forecasting human behavior. According to the program description, "work will focus on computational/analytical anthropological data collection, theory development, and application methodologies and tools" for creating software "to allow decision makers (intelligence analysts, operations analysts, operations planners, wargamers) to have available forecasting tools for socio-cultural (human terrain) responses at the strategic, operational, and tactical levels." Furthermore, HSCB "will provide data infrastructure/frameworks that will facilitate... visualization infrastructures [i.e. visually based technologies] to rapidly assess the human terrain at strategic to tactical levels."

Another crucial goal of HSCB is forecasting the effects of US military actions on native peoples. Or in other words, the "creation of validated, human terrain forecasting models that enable examination of 2nd, 3rd, and higher order effects of kinetic and non-kinetic actions within a theater in support of Effects Based Operations." According to the HBSC description, such "work will provide DoD capability to model intended or unintended political, military, economic, societal, infrastructure, and information effects of military actions."

As a former student of mechanical engineering, I am familiar with the tendency for practitioners in such fields to display a certain level of technological hubris. The idea that technicians can predict human behavior based on a set of variables reveals an overly simplistic understanding of the complexity of *Homo sapiens*.

"Visualization of Socio-cultural Information": MAP-HT and SNA

Several sources indicate that HTTs will make use of a software program called "Mapping the Human Terrain" or MAP-HT. As noted in Chapter 3, Kipp and his colleagues suggest that data collected by HTTs will be recorded on computers equipped with MAP-HT, which in turn will be transmitted to a centralized database accessible by other US government agencies—and eventually by the Iraqi and Afghan governments.

Various Pentagon documents also reveal the presence of the program, and provide additional information about its functions. In April 2007, the Defense Department announced its Joint Capability Technology Demonstration "new starts"—seven new projects aimed at moving advanced technologies into the battlefield. According to the announcement, MAP-HT represents "visualization of socio-cultural information" and

> seeks to demonstrate an integrated, open-source, spatially/relationally/temporally referenced human terrain data collection and visualization toolkit that helps combat teams understand the cultural context in which they must operate. Such understanding will help reduce explosive device incidents by optimizing the commander's operational decision-making process in a way that best harmonizes unit actions with the local culture.

The development of MAP-HT coincides with the DoD's urgent efforts to create a map of the human terrain. In an unclassified document dated August 2006, Pentagon staff reported:

> operations depend on the military's ability to operate effectively in a foreign society... one of the most important intelligence objectives is to ensure that operators in the field have knowledge of host populations: social structure (ethnic groups, tribes, elite networks, institutions, organizations and the rela-

tionships between them), culture (roles/statuses, social norms and sanctions, beliefs, values, and belief systems), cultural forms (myths, narratives, rituals, symbols), and power and authority relationships. This information must be appropriately linked to geospatial coordinates and provide a basic map of the human terrain that will improve the operational effectiveness of US forces.

By February 2007, the Office of the Secretary of Defense's (OSD) budget draft provided a more explicit description of MAP-HT:

The outcome of MAP-HT is to develop an integrated, open source, spatially/relationally/temporally referenced human terrain data collection and visualization toolkit to support BCT/RCTs [brigade combat teams/regimental combat teams] in understanding human terrain. The objective is to deploy MAP-HT toolkit to Joint, Interagency, Intergovernmental, and Multinational (JIMM) elements (e.g. USAID, DEA, Coalition Partners)... MAP-HT will provide a joint common relevant picture of the human terrain for use by tactical elements, operational commanders, theater planners, interagency organizations, and coalition partners... The overall project context for MAP-HT is development and deployment "by, through, and with" deployed units in contact... In addition to Army support, the US Marine Corps sees substantial merit in an institutionalized human terrain capability... A capability (people, process, and tools) must be further developed to provide a means for commanders and their supporting operations sections to collect data on human terrain, create, store, and disseminate information from this data, and use the resulting understanding as an element of combat power.

According to the OSD, $4.5 million will be needed between fiscal years 2007 and 2009 to support this "element of combat power."

Two companies named in the OSD draft budget—the MITRE Corporation (a federally funded research corporation) and Aptima—have each mentioned working on "human terrain." MITRE's 2005 Annual Report made a fleeting reference, noting that "MITRE is working with the Commands to address the insurgency problem on a number of fronts," namely "staff[ing] special data mining cells," and proto-typing "capabilities for ground units to increase under-standing of the tribal relationships and other aspects of the 'human terrain' in Iraq." (The MITRE Corporation did not respond to a request for more information.)

In a similar vein, Aptima's web page notes that the "enemy of today derives its power not from the size and strength of its military, but from its diffuse struc-

Figure 9. Mapping Iraq's human terrain during an air assault mission near the Zaghytun Chay River, November 2007. (Photo courtesy of US Department of Defense.)

ture, elusiveness, and adaptability," and that "counter-ing this new enemy requires a shift in strategy and tactics to focus on the 'human terrain'—the territory that Aptima knows best." Aptima claims that it can help clients "understand the culture and values of the civilian populations in which terrorist networks are embedded," and to "penetrate and disrupt the structure of terrorist organizations using computational models of the web of relationships that tie these networks together." Among Aptima's current products is its "Social Network Analysis" (SNA) software, developed in conjunction with Carnegie Mellon University. SNA "draws on state-of-the-art social science, psychology, and economic theories of human behavior" and has been used by the US military "to predict a state's poten-tial for instability or civil unrest in terms of nine key factors" ranging from "lack of essential services" to "corruption level" to "tension."

Although these descriptions of MAP-HT sound impressive, some people report a different real-ity. According to former HTT member Zenia Helbig—who underwent four weeks of HTT training in summer 2007—MAP-HT was cumbersome and rife with problems. (She noted that the program was developed by the MITRE Corporation, which is consistent with the DoD descriptions mentioned above.) In a training exercise conducted near Ft. Hood, Texas, some HTT members reportedly had to carry two laptop computers because those dedicated to running MAP-HT software were unable to conduct other tasks—overall, the system was far too special-ized. Helbig told me that what HTT members needed most were basic features such as wireless Internet access and Google maps, yet they had to lug around an extra laptop in order to meet this need. She described MAP-HT as a program with the capability of mapping relationships, events, places, times, and people. In theory, the goal is to draw connections between these things. In practice, MAP-HT is, in her words, "pointless." Another HTS employee—speaking on condition of anonymity—told me that the program is "sitting on a shelf." These allegations should spur US House and Senate Armed Service Committees into action, but so far it appears that these bodies have not made oversight of HTS and MAP-HT a high priority.

"Snake Eaters" and BATS: Surveillance of Human Terrain

Others seek to employ human terrain mapping for more efficient surveillance of Iraqis and Afghans by applying policing techniques and technologies. For example, in early 2007, elements from the US Marine Corps adopted a portable computerized ID system called "Snake Eater" (in reference to the name given to insurgents by the Marines), a battlefield version of an ID system originally developed for the Chicago Police Department. It consists of a mobile fingerprint scanner, an iris and retina scanner, a digital camera, GPS (global positioning system) software, and a laptop computer. According to a recent description, biometric data (for example, fingerprints and retina scans) collected by Snake Eater is transmitted to a "tactical operations center" and then to a server containing a database of the local population. There are plans to then send it to the FBI's biometric information database in Clarksburg, West Virginia.

Snake Eater's proponents draw comparisons between Iraqi insurgents and urban criminals in the US, in a manner reminiscent of the House Un-American Activities Committee's fearful assessment of America's alleged "guerrilla warfare advocates" (see Chapter 2):

> Iraq and Afghanistan find themselves torn by insurgency, sectarian violence, and terrorism. Instead of gang violence, warlords, tribes, sectarian death squads, and terrorist cells dominate urban landscapes akin to New York and Chicago. Instead of drugs alone, terrorist financing includes narcotics, extortion, and highly developed financial networks using porous borders and symbiotic affiliations to protect major actors.

They propose a technological fix for the insurgency that employs human terrain mapping for maintaining a blacklist, but also for psychological operations, according to *Joint Force Quarterly*: "[Snake Eater] saw action in Iraq and not only proved its direct impact on mapping human terrain, but also provided an undeniable psychological effect on a previously burgeoning insurgency." The plan would merge military actions with civilian policing.

US Marine Corps Major Owen West, who introduced the system in Iraq, commented to the *Wall Street Journal* about how it would enable his troops to emulate the "enemy":

> We're fixated on the enemy, but the enemy is fixated on the people. They know which families are apos-

tates, which houses are safe for the night, which boys are vulnerable to corruption or kidnapping. The enemy's population collection effort far outstrips ours. The Snake Eater will change that, and fast.

Snake Eater resembles the Biometrics Automated Toolkit System (BATS), a product developed by the military contract firm Northrop Grumman. Snake Eater, like BATS, enables soldiers to register fingerprints, facial scans, and iris patterns into a widely accessible database. According to one of its manufacturers, the Virginia-based Oberon Associates, BATS is "quickly finding its way closer to the tip of the military spear. BAT is a weapon system that has been instrumental in the War on Terror. It gives troops the ability to achieve identity dominance in the realm of force protection and combat operations."

Figure 10. US Marine Lance Corporal Luis Molina uses the Biometrics Automated Toolkit System (BATS) to scan the retina of a man in Fallujah, Iraq in January 2005. (Photo courtesy of US Army.)

Will HTTs begin using Snake Eater or BATS in the near future? It seems doubtful, given the importance of MAP-HT as the preferred HTT toolkit. But one thing is certain: the human terrain concept has taken hold across the military-industrial complex, including among those developing new technologies for "identity dominance"—which might more accurately be called control through human surveillance. As the US military undertakes more of what *The Economist* magazine candidly called "imperial policing" (known in military jargon as "Phase 4: Stability Operations"), it is predictable that they will begin using tactics and technologies borrowed from law enforcement agencies.

Role Playing and Video Gaming

Across some regions of the military landscape, computerized role playing exercises and video games are already being put to use. For example, the US Army's National Training Center (NTC) in Fort Irwin, California has developed software called "Reactive Information Propagation Planning for Lifelike Exercises" (or RIPPLE) to increase and improve battlefield intelligence—in other words, human terrain information:

> RIPPLE is network-modeling and artificial intelligence software that tracks all role players, roles, and relationships among the 1600 Iraqi role players. It maps all social, familial, and business relationships in the scenario as well as each role player's personal history and motivation. Based on this mapping the

NTC [National Training Center] can dynamically assess and model the effects of [US] unit interaction with Iraqi role players.

To make its simulation as realistic as possible, NTC has employed Hollywood producers, directors, actors, and special-effects technicians who have helped the NTC in developing scripts and scenarios, training role players, building physically realistic towns and villages, and creating explosive special effects (see Chapter 2).

The Air Force Research Lab has requested new proposals for modeling programs, and suggests that "researchers should investigate cultural, motivational, historical, political, and economic data to determine if there are mathematical and statistical models that can be used to predict the formation of terrorist activities." According to the proposal, the "goal is to determine sets of actions that can influence the root cause behaviors and cultivate a culture that does not support the development of criminal activity," an objective that effectively puts the Air Force in the business of social engineering.

The Office of Naval Research has requested proposals for a simulation tool resembling a video game:

> We are looking for innovative ideas that explore and harness the power of "advanced" interactive multimedia computer games (e.g. "sim games")... [incorporating] the best-practices of the videogame industry, including intuitive controls, story-telling, user-feedback... scenario editing, and high quality graphics & sound.

The Navy also issued a separate request for "rapid ethnographic assessment," which illustrates how human terrain data might fit into ongoing projects:

> The aim is to better understand the socio-cultural context in which these military missions operate... [Rapid Ethnographic Assessment] will ensure that military analysts will not just collect data, but also be able to know what data matters, in order to make sense of tribal, ethnic, and social class relationships, understand environmental factors (for example, the control of water in arid climates), land rights, disputes, the role of religion in everyday life, and the structure of the elites... Candidate methodologies include: cognitive anthropology, social network analysis, other methodologies with a structuralist focus, linguistics, applied anthropology, development anthropology, and computational approaches... it is expected that the proposal writer concentrate on one, significant scenario in one, actual culture. Example: Power structure in Afghanistan, Tribal structure and political affiliation in Sudan, Humanitarian relief in Pakistan, Reconstruction in Iraq.

It is not difficult to imagine scenarios in the near future in which agents use cultural profiles, social network analyses, and "visualization of the human terrain" for pre-emptive targeting of statistically probable (rather than actual) insurgents or extremists in Iraq, Afghanistan, Pakistan or other countries deemed to be terrorist havens.

Some Pentagon officials have already begun contemplating such applications. In February 2007, a dazzlingly illustrated PowerPoint presentation was released, which unambiguously stated a need to "'Map the Human Terrain' across the kill chain—enables the entire kill chain for the GWOT [Global War on

Terror]." The presentation (by Assistant Deputy Undersecretary of Defense James Wilcox) notes that "[s]ometimes we ID the enemy but... do not have an adequate/appropriate Strike Solution in time," indicating that at least one senior Pentagon official sees such information as a useful weapon.

Technicians of Power?

It is worth considering what the future holds once technologies like MAP-HT, HSCB, and SEAS are perfected, expanded, and incorporated into the military arsenal. At the time of writing, Lockheed Martin's

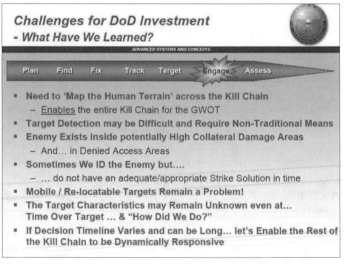

Figure 11. Mapping the human terrain "enables the entire kill chain," as asserted in this unclassified presentation by John Wilcox, Assistant Deputy Undersecretary of Defense. Wilcox made the presentation at the DoD's "Precision Strike Winter Roundtable," February 1, 2007. (Image courtesy of US Department of Defense.)

Advanced Technology Laboratories was advertising a position for a "Senior Situation Understanding Researcher-Human Terrain Analysis." The official job description notes that

> the successful candidate will be capable of leading a multidisciplinary, applied-research team defining and developing new human terrain characterization techniques contributing to military assessment of unfamiliar ethnic and tribal groups in preparation for winning the hearts and minds of foreign populations.

Furthermore, it stipulates that the candidate must have a PhD or masters degree and experience in "intelligence preparation of the battlespace, social network analysis, anthropology, decision aiding, or data mining for human-centered relationships" as well as "experience in planning, proposing and executing funded research and development projects in human terrain or social network analysis."

Are these the kinds of uses to which a democratic society should put its most talented minds—to "military assessment of unfamiliar ethnic and tribal groups" for "data mining," "winning the hearts and minds of foreign populations," and "preparation of the battlespace"? Should social scientists use expert knowledge for social engineering, manipulation, and targeting of people living in societies under illegal occupation by the US?

At the height of the Cold War, Columbia University sociologist C. Wright Mills cautioned social scientists about the perils of succumbing to the "bureaucratic ethos" and the "military metaphysic." He warned that "its use has been mainly in and for nondemocratic areas of society—a military establishment, a corporation." He was also concerned about the rapid transformation of scientists into mere technicians of power, lacking any sense of social responsibility for their actions. As those prosecuting the "war on terror" attempt to draw social scientists into ill-conceived operations, we should reaffirm our democratic values, our professional autonomy, and our social responsibility by refusing to participate.

Chapter 5
Social Science and
the Imperial Imperative

Scholars, who pride themselves on speaking their minds, often engage in a form of self-censorship which is called "realism." To be "realistic" in dealing with a problem is to work only among the alternatives which the most powerful in society put forth. It is as if we are all confined to a,b,c, or d in a multiple-choice test, when we know there is another possible answer. American society, although it has more freedom of expression than most societies in the world, thus sets limits beyond which respectable people are not supposed to think or speak.
                                        —Howard Zinn (1967)

How would *you* feel if you were an Iraqi being interviewed by some tall American guy with a soldiers' uniform and a gun? Something just doesn't seem right about it. The Iraqi doesn't have a choice. An anthropologist shouldn't study people who don't want to be studied.

A student at my university, after seeing photos of an embedded anthropologist wearing camouflage fatigues and a sidearm strapped to his leg, continued questioning me: "Is he *really* doing social science? Seems to me he's doing something else."

The student's comments get to the heart of a fundamental problem with HTS. The program does nothing to ensure that the concerns or the safety of Iraqis, Afghans, and other research participants are taken into account. There is no way of knowing whether an Iraqi would voluntarily agree to be interviewed under the circumstances.

Not allowing Iraqis to grant voluntary informed consent is a violation of the Nuremberg Code, which was crafted to discourage scientists from doing work that puts human research participants in harm's way. Among other things, the Code stipulates that before participating as a subject, the research participant should "be able to exercise free power of choice, without the intervention of any element of force, fraud, deceit, duress, over-reaching, or other ulterior form of constraint or coercion." The Code was written in reaction to depraved experiments that Nazi physicians carried out on hapless subjects during the 1940s.

The Uses and Abuses of HTS

But there are other problems with the program as well, for HTS—and the data collected by HTTs—perform a wide range of functions simultaneously. Images and news articles depicting a "gentler" counterinsurgency serve as propaganda for US audiences opposed to military operations in Iraq and Afghanistan, especially "liberal" audiences who might want to believe that US policies are not all bad. Like any propaganda, news reports covering HTS appeal to emotions through accounts that portray social scientists as selfless humanitarian miracle workers. They offer the apparently wonderful compromise of fighting a war that makes us feel good about ourselves.

Public relations campaigns that portray HTT personnel as life-saving heroes are also attracting young scholars who want to do good, not unlike civil servants who administered the British or French colonies. Instead of donning pith helmets and khaki clothing, today's neocolonial administrators wear pixelated camouflage uniforms and combat helmets, but the idea is the same: to help buttress "host nation" governments allied with the empire. For several years, there have been relatively few jobs for newly minted social science PhDs, and the six-digit salaries earned by HTT members are attractive.

There are plans underway to feed information collected by HTTs into a database accessible to the CIA, the Iraq police, or the Afghan military for strategic or tactical intelligence, or for use in targeting suspected insurgents for abduction or assassination. The lessons of the Phoenix Program should be clear: databases easily become blacklists in wartime situations, and innocent people face the danger of being misidentified as enemies. Innocent people also face the risk of being falsely accused by people with personal vendettas. The Vietnam War experience should serve as a warning to those who would share such databases with the Iraqi or Afghan governments, military, or police forces. The risk of abuse is great, particularly when social scientists gather data on kinship and social networks.

An interview I conducted with a former HTT member was especially disturbing. The person expressed grave concern about the possibility that data collected by social scientists about Iraqis would be mismanaged or misrouted. The identities of interviewees might be revealed, along with detailed information about their lives. Given the serious mismanagement of the program, the former HTT member saw this as a real possibility, though even efficient management of the program would still present grave ethical problems.

Historically, military personnel have employed cultural information to design psychological operations or propaganda campaigns. Will HTS data be used to exploit regionally-specific fears and vulnerabilities? There is nothing to indicate that "cultural data from hundreds of categories" wouldn't be used in harsh psychological operations campaigns.

How to Rent a Tribe

Another problem with HTS is that knowledge about local political hierarchies can facilitate the process of co-opting regional strongmen ("tribal sheiks" in Iraq; "warlords" in Afghanistan) in order to divide (and conquer) the population, and to facilitate indirect rule—a form of control in which a colonial power incorporates native institutions into the empire's framework.

The Ottoman, British and French empires employed divide-and-conquer policies in the late 19th and early 20th century, and the US military has begun employing a similar strategy today. The clearest indication of this comes from an analysis of western Iraq's "tribes": the 390-page *Iraq Tribal Study: al-Anbar Governorate*, released in summer 2006. The Pentagon commissioned the report, which was authored by a group consisting of former military intelligence officers (including one with a masters' degree in Middle East studies and anthropology); a retired US Army psychological operations officer; a former researcher for the Lincoln Group PR firm; a cultural anthropologist whose doctoral research focused upon counterinsurgency in Northern Ireland; and a US Army officer with a doctorate in international relations. The document reportedly circulated among officers at the Army's Command and General Staff College at Fort Leavenworth, Kansas when Petraeus was commanding general there.

Iraq Tribal Study focuses upon three groups ("tribes"): Albu Fahd, Albu Mahal and Albu Issa. The objectives of the document are stated in several chapter titles, particularly "Emerging Insights on Influencing the Tribes of al-Anbar" and "Example Application: Influencing the Three Target Tribes." The study reads like a handbook: there are instructions for how to "Leverage Traditional Authority," "Use a Compelling Ideology," "Use Appropriate Coercive Force," and "Use Economic Incentives and Disincentives," among others. In addition, the authors describe "How to Persuade the Tribes to Stop Supporting Insurgency," "How to Persuade the Tribes to Support the Coalition," and "How to Work and Live with Tribesmen."

The study frankly discusses the benefits of renting "tribes." For example, the authors review the period of Ottoman rule and the British Mandate for clues on adapting imperial techniques to the 21st century. A section entitled "Engaging the Shaikhs: British Successes, Failures, and Lessons" states:

> Convincing the shaikhs that the British were the dominant force... had a powerful effect... Subsidies

and land grants bought loyalty... Controlling water (irrigation canals), the economic lifelines of the shaikhs' constituencies was a powerful lever as well. It may be useful to examine the tribal landscape for modern parallels to the irrigation canals of the Mandate period... The key lies in putting into the shaikh's hands the ability to improve their people's livelihoods, and thereby the shaikh's own status.

The authors describe how the British handled recalcitrant sheiks:

the British were successful in their use of force against the tribes... Punitive assaults, both by infantry column and with air strikes, on the villages of shaikhs judged uncooperative brought about short-term cooperation and long-term enmity. Enabled largely by airpower, the British were able to stay in Iraq—with minimal resources—through its independence in 1932 and beyond.

They note how Baathist techniques might be emulated for social control:

The Baath regime fostered competition between tribes in a "divide and rule" campaign. This method was, and remains, effective because it exploits tribal honor and competition over limited resources. Competition between tribes can be a compelling way to secure the cooperation of one tribe at the expense of another. A tribe is likely to cooperate to keep another tribe from getting the benefits.

By the end of the study, the authors are more direct about manipulating Iraqis, and outline strategies for bribing: "Iraq's tribal values are ripe for exploitation. According to an old Iraqi saying, 'You cannot buy a tribe, but you can certainly rent one'... Shaikhs have responded well to financial incentives."

Iraq Tribal Study is sometimes schizophrenic. Occasionally the authors include passages espousing cultural relativism. For example, they note that "RESPECT (Ihtiram in Arabic) is the key to working with tribesmen anywhere in the world," and suggest that readers "Do not assume that they want to be like you" and "Do not reject their ways as primitive or backward." On the other hand, the authors often portray Arabs and Islam in unflattering and stereotypical terms: they solemnly comment upon "the fatalistic outlook that pervades Iraqi and Arab society," state that "Iraqi Arabs are generally submissive and obedient to their superiors" and suggest that Islam is characterized by a "medieval mind set... in which change is neither beneficial nor virtuous." Each of these statements demon-

Figure 12. "Tribal engagement" or indirect rule? US Army Lieutenant General Ray Odierno negotiates with a group of local leaders in the town of Owesat, western Iraq in December 2007. (Photo courtesy of US Army.)

strates a poor understanding of Arabic culture and Islam.

The First Time as Tragedy...

Like many government and military officials, the authors take an overly positivist view of "tribes," assuming that they are mappable, bounded groups with little membership change. Such an exaggerated view has serious consequences. For example, the authors scarcely mention how supporting Sunni "tribes" might facilitate sectarian violence against al-Anbar's Shia minority. Nor do they indicate how supporting Sunnis might destabilize a Shia-led government. Nor is there any substantive analysis of US officials' roles in the hardening of ethnic, sectarian and "tribal" boundaries. *Iraq Tribal Study* is so focused upon the internal structure and characteristics of "tribes" that there is negligible consideration of connections between these groups, the national government, and occupation forces.

While some may dismiss criticism of *Iraq Tribal Study* (after all, it is not ethnography but a "set of analytic and operational tools" according to the authors), it is worth considering how militarized social science has promoted shortsighted policies. The study reportedly informed Petraeus' strategy of encouraging US commanders to pay off (or bribe) Sunni power brokers who stood up against al-Qaeda operatives—a phenomenon now known as the al-Anbar "awakening." When Petraeus appeared before the US Congress to provide testimony regarding the situation in Iraq in

September 2007, he pointed to the "awakening" as an example of progress:

> The most significant development in the past six months likely has been the increasing emergence of tribes and local citizens rejecting al-Qaeda and other extremists. This has, of course, been most visible in Anbar Province. A year ago the province was assessed as "lost" politically. Today, it is a model of what happens when local leaders and citizens decide to oppose al-Qaeda and reject its Taliban-like ideology... We have, in coordination with the Iraqi government's National Reconcilia-tion Committee, been engaging these tribes and groups of local citizens who want to oppose extremists.

By the spring of 2008, Petraeus' "tribal engagement" strategy—which has paid out $767 million to mostly Sunni groups, with another $450 million on the way—was in full swing. Although US commercial media generally portrayed this as a success, critics argue that it is a reckless policy and potentially disastrous over the long run. Documentary film maker Rick Rowley was embedded with US troops in 2007 and observed the process:

> Through a combination of threats and enticements like releasing their kids from prison, the US military has gotten [Sunni] groups to join a coalition. They're paid money for small construction projects, and they're eventually incorporated into the Iraqi police force, where they're armed and paid, given a gun, a badge and the power to arrest... I didn't see anyone give an M16 to anyone. But I did see a US captain hand wads of cash to militiamen who were guarding checkpoints.

Support for the "tribes" has evidently entailed support for some of Iraq's "worst war criminals":

> In the town of Fallahat, where there used to be a lot of Shia, there are now no Shia... [We] found them living on the outskirts of Baghdad in a refugee camp... There are no services, no doctors, no hospitals, no schools, no running water, no work, no sanitation... The refugees we talked to knew the names of the people who have kicked them out and bombed their houses. And they are exactly the same tribes the Americans are working with... Maliki's head of negotiations with Sunni groups told us the groups the Americans are working with include some of the country's worst war criminals.

According to Rowley: "The US is funding sectarian militias fighting in a civil war in order to momentarily decrease attacks on Americans... It's an easy way to produce immediate statistical successes on the ground, a decrease in attacks on American soldiers." Rowley's comments indicate that a short-term strategy of supporting both sides in a civil war is undermining the long-term viability of the country.

Others warn that US support for the "awakening" is aggravating conflict between and among Sunni and Shia groups. Juan Cole suggests that US forces are creating a situation comparable to the Lebanese civil war of the 1970s and 1980s. Like the Syrians, who invaded and kept tens of thousands of troops in Lebanon through years of sectarian violence (while pitting Lebanese factions against each other), the US is unable or unwilling to end Iraq's civil war. From this perspective al-Anbar's "awakening" seems less like counterinsurgency and more like a high stakes divide-

and-conquer initiative enabled (or given an aura of legitimacy) by "social science." The similarities of this approach to colonial-era tactics employed in Northern Ireland, India, Rwanda, and Vietnam should give pause to those concerned about Iraq's future.

In the meantime, *Newsweek* magazine recently reported without a trace of irony that "Petraeus says he instructs his young officers, 'Go watch *The Sopranos* in order to understand the power dynamics at work in Iraq.'"

History repeats itself, "the first time as tragedy, the second time as farce."

In the Service of Empire

It doesn't take much imagination to envision how HTS connects with *Iraq Tribal Study*. (In fact, HTS architects Montgomery McFate and Andrea Jackson are among the authors of *Iraq Tribal Study*.) Both give priority to the needs and objectives of the US military—needs and objectives designed to encompass war fighter support, intelligence collection, counterinsurgency operations, and functions euphemistically referred to as "stability operations." Social science has given way to the imperial imperative.

What if we take the claims of HTS proponents at face value? Let's suppose that embedded Human Terrain teams (HTTs) are providing cultural expertise about Iraq and Afghanistan for US brigade commanders—and nothing more. Even under these circumstances, HTS represents a gross misuse of science. First, it denies guarantees that should be extended to all people approached by social scientists: the right to privacy and self-determination. Second, it transforms social science into a tool of manipulation and repression, by treating local people as pawns in a political game of neocolonial control over resource rich regions.

HTS represents a rejection of the enlightened role that Senator William Fulbright once envisioned. Social scientists, he said, "ought to be acting as responsible and independent critics of their government's policies." Instead, HTS advances the interests of a neocolonial power: it takes for granted the assumption that that US politicians, military commanders, and administrators have the right to decide what is best for Iraqis and Afghans; the notion that American lives are worth more than Iraqi lives; and the moral acceptability of the US-led military occupation in Iraq. In essence, its participants serve as technicians of empire.

Although US politicians still haven't come to terms with the notion of an American Empire, there is wide acceptance of the idea among historians, anthropologists, political scientists, and others from all sides of the political spectrum. Niall Ferguson, a controversial historian of the British Empire, famously noted that the US is an empire in all respects save one: "It is an empire, in short, that dare not speak its name. It is an empire in denial." Political scientist Jeffrey E. Garten has suggested that the US president create a "Colonial Service" for administering Iraq, Afghanistan, and other countries coping with "the aftermath of US military intervention."

Politicians' unwillingness to acknowledge empire means that to some degree, debates about HTS have framed the issue incorrectly. Instead of debating whether or not social scientists should be doing embedded military work, or whether such work is tactically effective, we should be asking whether participating in American imperialism and legalized plunder is acceptable today.

Social scientists have tread upon the imperial path before. To get a better understanding of the pitfalls connected with social science in the service of empire, the historical record can provide insight.

Southeast Nigeria, 1929

Late in 1929, thousands of indigenous Igbo women spontaneously rioted in southeastern Nigeria, then a colony of the British Empire. The women blocked roads, set fire to buildings, assaulted chiefs, and challenged troops sent by the government to restore order. The uprising lasted for several weeks, but not before colonial forces killed approximately 50 people.

The "Women's Riots" have been explained as the result of an increasingly oppressive tax system and a steep drop in the price of palm products, the key source of income for local people. (For years, British companies had relied upon palm oil exported from Nigeria, Malaya, and other colonies to lubricate industrial machinery throughout the empire.) But Igbo women also rebelled against the despised "Native Administration" which the British had installed in the region, a political system which established "Native Courts" managed by corrupt chiefs—local men who effectively served as powerful lackeys. The idea behind this system of indirect rule was to minimize the costs of maintaining political and economic control by co-opting local leaders who would collect taxes, resolve local conflicts, and manage affairs on behalf of the British.

Once the women's rebellion was smothered, the British government began investigating its causes and possible ways to prevent such occurrences in the future. They sought the assistance of C.K. Meek, a social anthropologist with more than 18 years of experience in northern Nigeria. According to Meek, he "was to deal with the Intelligence reports from the point of view of applied anthropology."

In his analysis, Meek argued that the chiefs and courts installed by the British were radically different from "village-councils" and other decentralized political arrangements that had existed in southeastern Nigeria during the pre-colonial period. He suggested that more nuanced and culturally appropriate forms of "Native Administration" might lead to a more stable situation in which "the Ibo advances along the path of political progress."

Meek's peers undoubtedly saw him as a liberal, since he advocated indirect (as opposed to direct) rule of Britain's African colonies. Furthermore, his sensitive description of "the vigour and intelligence of the Ibo people, which have made them one of the largest and most progressive tribes in Africa" must have appeared remarkably sympathetic in the eyes of many Britons. Yet in the end, Meek was unable to envision Igbo life beyond the British empire. He was fully aware that the government's attitude towards anthropology was that it should serve as the "handmaiden to administration" by providing data that would help the government "make the fullest use of Native institutions as instruments of local administration." Meek's work paternalistically denied from the outset the possibility of Ibo self-determination. Underlying his work was the notion that Africans were unable to adapt to the modern world without British protection.

Meek was hardly alone in seeing colonialism's inevitability, or indirect rule as the best option for European control of African colonies. S.F. Nadel, a leading figure in social anthropology, was also a strong proponent. When, in the late 1930s, British government officials recruited Nadel to help control Nuba peoples in what was then the Anglo-Egyptian Sudan, he eagerly accepted. According to Nadel, his study "was primarily planned to be of practical value to administrators and others." He noted that the government considered the Nuba to be

> powerfully affected by the authority of the Government, the forces of economics and the influence of science... Their lives were still largely conditioned by superstitions and customs imperfectly known to the administration... Keen officials, especially technical officials, were apt to override native customs rather than make use of them.

For Nadel, making use of Nuba customs included establishing "Native Courts" with "Government-sponsored Chieftainships"—that is, indirect rule. (Two years later, problems with the courts led government troops to drive the Jebel Tullushi indigenous group out of their mountain homes.)

Like Meek, Nadel was incapable of envisioning Africa beyond colonialism, or to see the role of the social scientist as anything other than "of practical value to administrators" seeking to control native peoples.

Such perspectives reveal these anthropologists' complicity in the colonial enterprise. Although Meek saw his role as a benevolent one, and Nadel argued that "the blunders of the anthropologists will be 'better' blunders," neither Meek, nor Nadel, nor dozens of other anthropologists challenged the assumption that colonizers had the right—and the obligation—to decide what was best for the natives.

In spite of many devastating critiques of colonial anthropology, today's HTS architects crassly argue that HTTs can promote the Phase 4 "stability goals" of the US military by co-opting local headmen—an objective reminiscent of the work of Meek and others charged with helping British colonial administrators develop "Native Administrations" in Nigeria and beyond. Today, the US government has no "colonial service" but by default, the Pentagon has been assigned many of the tasks required to maintain the American Empire. It is not surprising under such circumstances that the Pentagon is contracting social scientists to help achieve these objectives.

Mesopotamia, 1920

Even earlier, archaeologists helped establish a de facto system of British colonial rule in Iraq (then called Mesopotamia) after World War I. Although the roles they played differed in some respects from the roles of Meek and Nadel, they were guided by the same basic assumptions: an enthusiasm for applying the tools of cultural familiarity for more effective control; the unquestioned assumption that European powers were exceptionally able at managing native peoples; a fundamental belief in the correctness of imperialism; a willingness to accept the limited number of policy options acceptable to powerful members of British society; and a lack of attention to the aspirations of native people for genuine self-rule.

T.E. Lawrence—immortalized as "Lawrence of Arabia" by the US media—is best known for helping to coordinate the so-called Arab Revolt against the Ottoman Turks beginning in 1916. But Lawrence was first drawn to the Middle East when he was given the opportunity to do archeology work in northern Syria under the tutelage of David George Hogarth. When World War I erupted, Lawrence eagerly lent his geographic expertise and familiarity with Arabic language and culture to the war effort. He was assigned to the British army in Cairo and soon began supplying money and weapons to Arab fighters led by Prince Feisal. (Feisal was the son of King Hussein, who ruled over the Hejaz—the lands surrounding the holy cities of Mecca and Medina.) Using guerrilla tactics such as dynamiting the vital Hejaz Railway, Lawrence's Arab allies disrupted Turkish supply lines throughout the Middle East. In 1917, they won a key victory at Aqaba, the site of a Turkish fort, and their efforts eventually helped British troops take Jerusalem and Damascus. By 1918, the British occupied all of modern-day Iraq.

Feisal's Arab fighters cooperated with the British after many assurances that they would be rewarded with political autonomy. For years, Lawrence and others sought to convince British government officials that a peculiar form of Arab "independence" would be beneficial. In a 1916 intelligence report, he noted that the Arab Revolt was:

beneficial to us, because it marches with our immediate aims, the break up of the Islamic "bloc" and the defeat and disruption of the Ottoman Empire, and because *the states [Sharif Hussein] would set up to succeed the Turks would be... harmless to ourselves...* The Arabs are even less stable than the Turks. *If properly handled they would remain in a state of political mosaic, a tissue of small jealous principalities incapable of cohesion.*

Writer and archaeologist Gertrude Bell, who had gained much respect among British commanders for her analyses of intelligence information about Arab groups who might be encouraged to join the revolt against Turks, was another supporter of Iraqi independence—of an odd sort. Bell attempted to persuade British officials that the facade of an administration could be created with competent local men—in other words, she proposed creating a controlled system of indirect rule.

Even so, she doubted that influential Shia clergy were up to the task, since they were "sitting in an atmosphere which reeks of antiquity and is so thick with the dust of ages that you can't see through it—nor can they." She feared the prospect of Shia leaders in a majority Shiite region; indeed, in 1920 she wrote: "The object of every government here has always been to keep the Shia divines from taking charge of public affairs." Perhaps it is for this reason that she declared: "Mesopotamia is not a civilized state."

The proposals offered by Lawrence and Bell didn't convince British government officials to grant Arabs autonomy after the League of Nations awarded Britain a mandate over Mesopotamia in 1920. Sunni and Shia understandably viewed the mandate as a form of colonialism since the British immediately imposed direct rule on the region, under the leadership of High Commissioner Sir Percy Cox. They quickly put aside their differences and rose up against their British masters. In the end, hundreds of British troops were killed in the uprising. The government eventually resorted to aerial bombing and the use of white phosphorus (a chemical that produces severe burns as well as liver, heart, and kidney damage) to put down the rebellion, killing nearly 10,000 Arabs in the process. (History repeated itself in November 2005, when Pentagon spokesman Barry Venable told BBC News that white phosphorus was "used as an incendiary weapon against enemy combatants" in Iraq.)

Figure 13. Gertrude Bell (in white dress) became a close advisor to High Commissioner Sir Percy Cox, who was charged with administering Mesopotamia during the period of the British mandate in the early 1920s. (Photo courtesy of US Library of Congress.)

By 1921, Winston Churchill (then British Secretary of State for the Colonies) consulted with Lawrence and Bell in Cairo, where they were vindicated: to save costs, the British established "a mixture of direct and indirect rule" based on the model of colonial India. They installed Feisal as the colony's monarch, which effectively created a puppet regime dependent on Great Britain politically and economically.

After Feisal was made king, Bell was assigned to the British High Commission advisory group in Baghdad. There she and Sir Percy Cox forged a series of divide-and-conquer policies that survived beyond the 20th century, including the use of Kurdish territory as a buffer against Turkey and Russia; the promotion of

Figure 14. Prince Feisal (center) and T.E. Lawrence (middle row, second from right) at the 1921 Cairo Conference. (Photo courtesy of the US Library of Congress.)

Sunni Muslims over the Shia majority; repression or expulsion of Shia clergymen in Najaf, Kerbala, and Kazimain; the buying off of big landowners and "tribal" elders; fraudulent elections; and deployment of air power for political control.

After 1932, when Iraq gained its nominal independence, British commanders were still given the right to maintain military bases in and move troops through Iraq. (By this point, the country was of great economic importance to the British because of its oil resources.) The Iraqi monarchy lasted as a client regime with little change until 1958.

A lesson to be learned from the work of Lawrence and Bell is that in the end, it is unlikely that an influential or well-informed social scientist will significantly impact decision makers pursuing imperial imperatives. Lawrence gained the trust of thousands of Arabs, lived among them for more than five years, spoke their language, and led them in battle against the Ottomans. He promised them autonomy after the war, but the Arabs were ultimately betrayed: British politicians extended direct rule over Mesopotamia.

Another lesson to take from the work of Lawrence and Bell is that the social scientist's perspective isn't necessarily opposed to that of colonial officials. Although both were probably considered "liberal" in the 1920s from a British perspective—after all, they advocated indirect rather than direct rule—the end result was not substantively different, from the Iraqi point of view. After King Feisal assumed power, British advisers in Baghdad still made key political and economic decisions, thousands of British troops remained in the region for decades, and the British-owned Iraqi Petroleum Company was granted full concessions over Iraqi oil. Like Meek and Nadel, both Lawrence and Bell maintained a paternalistic view that took for granted the necessity of European intervention in the affairs of people deemed less than civilized—a pattern of positional superiority and plunder being repeated today in the Middle East region.

It is tempting to condemn Meek, Nadel, Lawrence, and Bell for their work, but they must be seen within the context of their time. Few of their peers dared to envision a world beyond colonialism—after all, they believed that Europeans were bringing the hallmarks of civilization to the colonies: schools, health clinics, modern science, and technology. It is easier to understand their actions if we consider the totalistic ideology of empire.

It is much more difficult to understand why today, some HTS participants are unfazed by anthropology's colonial roots. For example, in mid-2007 Marcus Griffin wrote: "Is the use of the anthropological perspective by the military promoting imperialism? Who can really say? Is anthropology antithetical to imperialism? Not if you look at the discipline's origins in colonialism in the late 1800s and early 1900s." Marcus' remarks are chilling: embedded military anthropology may promote empire ("Who can really say?"), but since the discipline has historical links to colonialism, that's OK.

Towards a Decolonized Social Science

As colonial anthropologists were hard at work in the 1920s and 1930s, a Kikuyu man from British East

Africa (now Kenya) arrived in London. During his time there, Jomo Kenyatta began attending seminars conducted by Bronislaw Malinowski, perhaps the best known European anthropologist of the time. Kenyatta was profoundly influenced by anthropology, and wrote a stirring ethnography of Kikuyu life entitled *Facing Mount Kenya* in 1938. Kenyatta had a clear vision for how social anthropology could be used as a tool for challenging—not supporting—colonial rule. His book began with a preface that was searingly critical of colonial officials and others claiming to be "friends of the African":

> In the present work I have tried my best to record facts as I know them, mainly through a lifetime of personal experience, and have kept under very considerable restraint the sense of political grievances which no progressive African can fail to experience... I know that there are many scientists and general readers who will be disinterestedly glad of the opportunity of hearing the Africans' point of view, and to all such I am glad to be of service. At the same time, I am well aware that I could not do justice to the subject without offending those "professional friends of the African" who are prepared to maintain their friendship for eternity as a sacred duty, provided only that the African will continue to play the part of an ignorant savage so that they can monopolise the office of interpreting his mind and speaking for him. To such people, an African who writes a study of this kind is encroaching on their preserves. He is a rabbit turned poacher.

Kenyatta then did something that neither Meek, nor Nadel, nor Lawrence, nor Bell were able to do: to envision a future beyond imperialism:

But the African is not blind. He can recognize these pretenders to philanthropy, and in various parts of the continent he is waking up to the realisation that a running river cannot be dammed for ever without breaking its bounds. His power of expression has been hampered, but it is breaking through, and will very soon sweep away the patronage and repression which surround him.

Kenyatta became an ardent activist, nationalist leader, and revolutionary. He was imprisoned for nearly a decade for his political activities. His ethnography examined the painful consequences of British colonialism from a Kikuyu perspective, and he inspired thousands of Africans, Europeans, and others to oppose the imperial imperative. He founded the Pan-African Federation with Kwame Nkrumah in 1946, an organi-

Figure 15. Jomo Kenyatta, first prime minister and president of Kenya, circa 1965. (Photo courtesy of the US Library of Congress.)

zation dedicated to promoting independence for African nations. He would go on to become the first Prime Minister and President of an independent Kenya in the 1960s.

Kenyatta's work demonstrates how the anthropologist need not play the role of servant to the most powerful in society. There are other options, other choices. Social science can just as effectively lead the way to a more democratic future. It is just as capable of challenging power as serving it.

Part of what made Kenyatta's work so powerful was that it gave a voice to those living under colonialism. It seems obvious that in the context of the US-led occupation of Iraq and Afghanistan, social scientists should insist that US government officials respect local sovereignty, and to listen to Iraqi and Afghan perspectives— not only the perspectives of elites, but of ordinary people.

In spite of their titles ("cultural analysts") HTT social scientists appear to be doing otherwise. They generally don't speak the languages of the Middle East and Central Asia. They are embedded with combat troops, they eat MREs (military rations), they sleep in military barracks, and they do not participate in the daily lives of Iraqis and Afghans. As embedded specialists they are by definition unable to conduct independent work.

What comes across from the accounts of many social scientists supporting counterinsurgency initiatives in Iraq and Afghanistan is a fundamental acceptance of modern warfare in general and the US-led occupations in particular. Furthermore, they generally accept the false notion that counterinsurgency—the "graduate level of war" to quote one military enthusiast—is more antiseptic, more humane, less damaging than conventional warfare. As technicians of power, some adhere strictly to Machiavellian principles: do not question the prince or his war, but instead use the most efficient means to help him achieve victory. War's inevitability is taken for granted. Basic assumptions are left unquestioned.

Missing from these accounts is the question of whether war is appropriate at all today. Missing are the observations of Albert Einstein, who convened a press conference in 1932 to declare: "War cannot be humanized. It can only be abolished." Missing too are the insights of renowned anthropologist Margaret Mead, who noted in 1940 that "Warfare is only an invention—not a biological necessity." In short, the Machiavellian mindset—and a studied disinterest in anthropological insights (which illustrate that some human societies never engaged in organized armed conflict)—stand as barriers to thinking new about a less violent world.

In both Afghanistan and Iraq today, one thing is clear. The means of war and occupation are predictable and certain—civilian casualties, indiscriminate violence, and needless suffering. The ends of war and occupation are unpredictable and not at all certain. Should social scientists continue to participate in employing such predictable means or seeking such unpredictable ends?

None of this is to deny the real threat of terrorism, or the existence of "bad guys" in the world today. But it is crucial to keep in mind the fact that states too engage in terrorism (including countries that receive billions of dollars annually from US taxpayers—Israel, Egypt, Pakistan, Colombia) and that all too often, "bad guys" have been strengthened by Washington's approval or support (Musharraf, Mubarak, Obiang, and Saud to name but a few). This isn't a new phenomenon; indeed, one need only remember how the Shah, Pinochet, Mobutu, Trujillo, Diem, Rios Montt, Suharto, Duvalier, Batista—and yes, Saddam Hussein and Osama bin Laden among many others—were "our SOBs" (to use FDR's phrase) for decades.

Rather than accept rhetorical arguments comparing the "war on terror" to World War II and other wars that are often held up as "just" wars, it is worth considering the words of historian Howard Zinn, who was an enthusiastic bombardier before he adopted a position of non-violence:

> Germany [in the 1940s] was an aggressive nation expanding its power... But today we do not face an expansionist power that needs to be appeased. We ourselves are the expansionist power that demands to be appeased. We ourselves are the expansionist power—troops in Saudi Arabia, bombings of Iraq, military bases all over the world, naval vessels on every sea—and that, along with Israel's expansion into the West Bank and Gaza Strip, has aroused anger... To get at the roots of terrorism is complicated... At the core of unspeakable and unjustifiable acts of terrorism are justified grievances felt by millions of people who would not themselves engage in terrorism but from whose ranks terrorists spring.

Those concerned about doing something to deal with terrorist threats might consider how more realistic solutions might include addressing root causes—the "justified grievances felt by millions"—rather than "surgical" air strikes, troop "surge" strategies, or new counterinsurgency programs after the damage has been done.

Turning the tide will require a better informed citizenry. Classrooms, town halls, newspapers, TV and radio programs, and the streets were once sites for democratic dialogue and debate in this country, and reclaiming them will be an essential part of demilitarizing the future. Change of this magnitude happens slowly, but those who care about making the world a less violent place in the long run are already hard at work.

Some anthropologists have provided tremendous insight for citizens beyond the academy, but not by embedding themselves with military units. For example, William Beeman (who first began doing research in Iran more than 30 years ago) recently reported:

> From the perspective of Iraqi Shi'ites, the United States is neither better nor worse than the British seventy years ago... If the United States now establishes its own puppet regime in Baghdad, the symbolic parallel with the British action after World War I will be complete, and nothing will be able to convince the skeptics in Iraq that the United States has any interest there except colonial domination.

Beeman's syndicated commentaries reach millions of Americans with vital cultural and historical information, and he has also addressed officers at the Naval Postgraduate School:

The Iraqis read the American "mandate" as the equivalent of the British Mandate. It is also seen as just as illegitimate... It should be obvious that the Iraqis are now revolting against the United States in a manner similar to the way that they revolted against Great Britain in 1920 and again in 1958, when the British were removed once and for all. The circumstances behind the revolt of 1920 and the revolution of 1958 are vastly different, but all three events stem broadly from a desire on the part of the Iraqis to strike out at what they see as oppression by an unwelcome outside power.

Unembedded independent journalists like Nir Rosen also provide the general public with a sense of how decolonized social science might challenge the assumptions of the new imperialists:

According to almost every Iraqi, the Americans "came as liberators and now they are occupiers." For Americans occupation conjures images of postwar Germany or Japan, and the repair of damaged societies. In Arabic, *tahir*, or liberation, and *ihtilal*, or occupation, have much greater moral and emotional significance. *Ihtilal* means the Crusaders who slaughtered Muslims, Jews, and Orthodox Christians, it means the Mongols who sacked Baghdad in the thirteenth century, it means the British imperialists who divided the spoils of the Ottoman Empire with the French, and it means the Israelis in southern Lebanon and Palestine.

Social scientists, particularly anthropologists, would be well served by forcefully communicating these ideas to the public. Such work, based upon on-the-ground experience and intimate cultural knowledge, suggests a novel approach in which social scientists might play a leading role: a preventive diplomacy that aims to forestall future crises by recognizing and addressing root causes of conflict—for example, the dangerous ideology of American exceptionalism (the idea that the US is substantively different from and superior to other countries), or the common features of the US occupation of Iraq and the Israeli occupation of the Palestinian territories.

This might be both public service and civic duty: to critique reckless US government policies; the relationships between government officials, the military establishment, and multinational corporations; and the effects and consequences of American Empire across the globe from the perspective of people whose lives are impacted by our country's actions. By appealing directly to the general public, a decolonized social science might inform ordinary people (as well as policy making elites) about how US foreign policy often creates new enemies abroad. Confronting persistent ignorance with persistent appeals to reason may lead to political change if public opinion can be impacted. Without the push and pull of ordinary citizens, there is no democracy.

In the future, historians may question why a small number of anthropologists and social scientists—whose forward-thinking predecessors developed the modern culture concept, critiqued Western ethnocentrism in its various guises, and invented the teach-in—decided to enlist as embedded specialists in an open-ended war of dubious legality. They might wonder why these scientists began harvesting data on Iraqis and Afghans as a preferred method of practical "real-world" engagement. They might ask why, at a time when large majorities in the US, Iraq, and Afghanistan called for the withdrawal of US troops, this group supported an occupation resulting in hundreds of thousands of civilian deaths.

Future historians might also be puzzled about some social scientists' failure to learn lessons from an earlier era. Quite apart from the example of the colonial anthropologists of the early 20th century, we might consider these words, as applicable today as when they were written in the midst of another neocolonial war, in Vietnam:

> When we strip away the terminology of the behavioral sciences, we see revealed, in work such as this, the mentality of the colonial civil servant, persuaded of the benevolence of the mother country and the correctness of its vision of world order, and convinced that he understands the true interests of those backward peoples whose welfare he is to administer.

The fact that some social scientists have warmly embraced HTS reveals historical amnesia, opportunism, and a profound lack of imagination. It is also symptomatic of an intellectual impoverishment plaguing our society.

To the extent that HTS uses "cultural knowledge" to create propaganda campaigns to win "'will and legitimacy' fights," it deserves condemnation. To the extent that HTS peddles social science techniques and concepts in support of conquest and indirect rule, it deserves rejection. To the extent that HTS might be employed to collect intelligence or target suspected enemies for assassination, the program deserves elimination—and a period of sober reflection about the situation of American social science today. ■

Glossary of Terms

AAA   American Anthropological Association

ARPA   Advanced Research Projects Agency; special
                  branch of US Department of Defense that
                  funds military research

BAE Systems   UK military contractor responsible for
                  recruiting, training, and administration
                  services for Human Terrain System

BATS   Biometrics Automated Toolkit System; tool
                  that allows the user to record fingerprints,
                  facial scans, and iris patterns

CACI   Consolidated Analysis Center, Inc.; US
                  military contractor whose subsidiary, the
                  Wexford Group, has recruited Human Terrain
                  Team members

CIA   US Central Intelligence Agency

COINTELPRO   Counterintelligence Program; secret FBI
                  program conducted in the late 1960s and
                  early 1970s to repress political dissent

CORDS   Civil Operations and Revolutionary
                  Development Support; Vietnam War-era
                  civil-military counterinsurgency initiative

DAGA   Dynamic Adversarial Gaming Algorithm;
                  computer program developed by researchers
                  at Dartmouth College to predict how
                  individuals or groups might react to political,
                  economic, and social events

DCGS   Distributed Common Ground System;
                  network of systems linking databases and
                  intelligence information from US military and
                  intelligence agencies

DoD	US Department of Defense
FMSO	Foreign Military Studies Office; US Army center specializing in regional military issues, located at Fort Leavenworth, Kansas
HSCB	Human Social and Culture Behavioral modeling; research program launched by the US Department of Defense to model and simulate human behavior using specialized computer programs
HTT	Human Terrain Team; five-person civilian-military team embedded with US Army in Iraq and Afghanistan for counterinsurgency work
HTS	Human Terrain System; experimental US Army counterinsurgency program
HUAC	House Un-American Activities Committee; committee of the US House of Representatives charged with investigating subversion and disloyalty from 1938 to 1975
IED	Improvised explosive device
MAP-HT	Mapping the Human Terrain; computerized database that allows the user to collect, store, and manipulate detailed cultural data; developed for use in the Human Terrain System program
MITRE	MITRE corporation; federally funded research and development corporation
MTC Technologies	Modern Technologies Corporation; US military contractor that recruits Human Terrain Team members
NEK	NEK Advanced Securities Group; US military contractor that recruits Human Terrain Team members

NTC	National Training Center; US Army training facility located at Fort Irwin, California
OSD	Office of the Secretary of Defense
OSS	US Office of Strategic Services; US intelligence agency created in the 1940s that was precursor to the CIA
PNAC	Project for the New American Century; neoconservative think tank founded in the early 1990s
RAND	Research and Development Corporation; federally funded research and development corporation
SCIA	Socio-Cultural Intelligence Analysis, Inc.; company that specializes in using social science for intelligence analysis
SEAS	Synthetic Environment for Analysis and Simulation; computerized modeling and simulation program developed at Purdue University
TRADOC	Training and Doctrine Command; US Army center responsible for training soldiers and developing military doctrine
UCMJ	Uniform Code of Military Justice; rules and regulations governing conduct of US military personnel, and provides the foundation of military law
USAID	United States Agency for International Development
VC	Viet Cong; term for Vietnamese communists during the Vietnam War
VCI	Viet Cong infrastructure; Vietnam War-era term for civilian supporters of Vietnamese communists

Acknowledgments

Many thanks to Laura Nader for her mentoring, collegiality, and friendship over the past 15 years; to David Price for his encouragement and careful reading of my work; to Gustaaf Houtman, editor of the journal *Anthropology Today*, for providing thoughtful reviews of two articles which have been incorporated into this text; and to Hugh Gusterson for his generosity and insightful comments. Matthew Engelke and Marshall Sahlins of Prickly Paradigm Press helped me improve the manuscript in many ways.

For their interest in my work (and their suggestions) I am grateful to Roberto, Imelda, Ernesto, and Jorge González; to Veronica Hyma, Adam Rodriguez, Eduardo Flores, and Khurram Tai; to colleagues from the Network of Concerned Anthropologists (Catherine Besteman, Andrew Bickford, Greg Feldman, Hugh Gusterson, Gustaaf Houtman, Jean Jackson, Kanhong Lin, Catherine Lutz, David Price, and David Vine); and to Barbara Rylko-Bauer. Finally, I am grateful to Heidi Kao for listening to the earliest draft, and for her constant encouragement and support. This book is dedicated to her.

Note: For information regarding source material and passages quoted in the text, contact the author at roberto_gonzalez@netzero.net.

Also available from Prickly Paradigm Press:

continued